P9-BZK-314

The Fabulous '50s

The Cars, The Culture

Edited by
John A. Gunnell
& Mary L. Sieber

© 1992 by Krause Publications
All rights reserved. No portion of this book
may be reproduced in any form without permission.

Published by

700 East State St.   Iola WI 54990

Library of Congress Catalog Number: 92-71454
ISBN: 0-87341-199-4
Printed in the United States of America

Acknowledgements

Sincere thanks go to *Old Cars Weekly* columnists Pat Chappell, Peter Winnewisser, John Lee, Bill Siuru Jr. and R. Perry Zavitz, as well as *Old Cars Weekly* free-lance writer Charles Webb, for their contributions to this book; to Don Chandler and Thomas Gunnell for the cover photo of the Thunderbird; to the Outdoor Advertising Association for the use of their billboards as art throughout this book; and to all those wonderful people who sent us pictures of their collector cars from the Fabulous '50s.

Contents

Introduction

By Pat Chappell

What a decade it was: the Fabulous '50s! A time for celebration; a time for expansion; a time for some of the most beautiful and most outlandish automobiles ever manufactured.

It was peace and prosperity; an era of magnificent excess; a decade of dazzle; a culmination of chrome dreams; a golden age of "Gorp." and much much more.

Almost 60 million vehicles were produced in the '50s, and they were ones we would always remember. One writer summed it up: "These cars brought forth spontaneous displays of passion." An auto journalist explained: "Styling was a tyrannical force in this era." And yet another told us, "Chrome was god, and Harley Earl was its prophet."

They were all right, of course. The excess and the glitter rose out of the long depression of the '30s; World War II and the complete absence of civilian car and truck manufacture for almost four years; and the wave of shortages and strikes which followed in the '40s. Then the initial postwar surge in the late '40s was hit head on by the Korean conflict in the early '50s. Finally, as restrictions and price controls were lifted by early '53, this powerful styling and production force which had been held back, yet was building up for so very long, was in motion. It was like a tide that knew no timetable, an explosion, an expansion that wouldn't quit.

Quite simply, during the '50s we created a society around our cars: suburbia; underpasses and freeways; drive-in movies, miniature golf and strip shopping centers; camping grounds and Mom and Pop motels; White Castles and other hamburger joints galore. America was on the go, and the American automobile was the vehicle of choice.

In the '50s our society came of age, and with it the auto industry, too. Buck Rogers' dream had come true. The future was now. The entire country was optimistic. One designer reminded us: "During the '50s the car was a romantic symbol. Manufacturers were putting style into car bodies. They were not just the vehicles for basic transportation. They were moving sculpture."

We had an expanding middle class. After making sacrifices during the '30s and '40s, we were ready to buy, buy, buy! We couldn't wait to go down to the auto dealer's showroom and see what was "new" each year. And we loved these machines and images of jets and rockets which had found a way into their design. These cars of the '50s were for us symbols of power and status. In many cases, particularly toward the end of the decade, we were looking for a second family car to display proudly in the driveway of our suburban split-level home with its two-car garage!

As the '50s began, ten companies were represented in the automobile industry: General Motors, Ford, Chrysler, Studebaker, Nash, Kaiser-Frazer, Hudson, Packard, Willys and Crosley. By 1959, all that remained were GM, Ford, Chrysler, American Motors (formed out of Nash and Hudson), and Studebaker (which had merged with Packard).

The independents that disappeared either by demise or merger in the '50s certainly made an impression on the buying public and, in retrospect, showed considerable innovation in automotive styling and engineering. Some felt that had these independents been more accurate in their aim at the powerful Big Three in their all-new efforts in the early '50s, things would be different today. Others felt that had a complete merger been a reality, the Big Three would have been the Big Four at least beyond the '50s and into the '60s. But it wasn't to be.

Alfred P. Sloan, CEO of GM for 23 years, had predicted that three important postwar developments would dominate the cars of the '50s: styling, high compression engines and automatic transmissions. His prophecy came true.

An overview of '50s automotive styling shows the conservative approach in the early '50s yielding to the glitz, dazzle and outlandish features of the late '50s. We are reminded of the power of Harley J. Earl, vice president of styling for General Motors, whose "lower, longer, wider" dictate influenced the rest of the automotive industry. His ever-lasting presence and his dynamic personality played an important role in the early postwar period, although others like Raymond Loewy of Studebaker, Virgil Exner of Chrysler, Frank Spring of Hudson, and John Reinhardt of Ford represented a formidable styling force as well.

A major influence on automotive styling in the '50s was to come from GM's traveling Motorama shows. Not only would the public in large cities throughout the United States see GM's "dream cars of the future" on display, but other automotive companies took copious notes on the corporation's experimental styling and engineering.

Certain body styles were evolving. One was the sporty-looking two-door hardtop, which would increase its market share from nine percent in 1951 to twenty-eight percent in 1959. Another popular body style was the station wagon. No longer was this a wood-bodied estate wagon for the wealthy only. In an all-metal version it was just the ticket for the middle class family in suburbia. Plymouth's all-metal 1949 Suburban wagon kicked off this revolution, and growth throughout the industry was phenomenal: from 1951's three percent of the market (174,000) to 1959's seventeen percent (almost one million).

Another popular body style was the sporty two-place vehicle. In 1953, Chevrolet's Motorama Corvette went into production, and to this day it survives to celebrate its 40th birthday and the millionth production milestone. Ford's entry into this field was the 1955 Thunderbird, which survived in its two-place form through 1957. From 1958 on, the Thunderbird has grown to become more of a personal car, a luxury sedan.

Soft top convertibles continued to be popular, and in the '50s they were available thoughout the industry. In 1949, convertibles represented four percent of the market. By 1959, they rose to five percent.

During the '50s, three styling manifestations developed which did more to make these cars memorable than anything elese. This trio of hallmarks reflected the wonderfully exhuberant postwar era: vibrant two- and sometimes three-tone exterior paints; excessive use of chrome, stainless and aluminum trim on auto bodies; and what started modestly, but grew to outlandishness, tailfins. Adding all this to a lower, longer and wider body resulted in an absolutely remarkable vehicle.

Flashy exteriors and color coordinated interiors were representative of the period. Combinations such as pink and gray, turquoise and ivory, and yellow and black wore well on these cars. These hues were also reflected in bathrooms, kitchens and restaurants of the era.

Brightwork in the form of chrome, stainless and aluminum was applied to cars tastefully in the early to mid '50s, but by 1958-'59 it looked, as one designer decribed, "like we laid it on with a trowel."

The famous tailfin, introduced by Cadillac in 1948 as a modest and graceful touch, grew and grew. Emphasized by Chrysler's Virgil Exner as that corporation's "forward look" which turned into the "finny look," fins became out-of-control rear appendages. But they are sure something to behold today.

Sloan's second prediction, that of the trend toward high compression engines, certainly came true in the '50s. Quite simply, with the cars longer, wider and heavier with a direction toward more and more options, the development of the more powerful V-8 engine, pretty much across the board in the mid '50s, had become a necessity. (In 1951, only twenty-nine percent of engines manufactured were V-8s — fifteen percent were straight eights. By 1959, seventy percent of engines manufactured were V-8s.) The great horsepower race, which started in 1951 when Chrysler's new V-8 outpowered Cadillac's, continued through the '50s, as the low-priced three (which all had V-8s by 1955) entered the race.

Sloan also predicted the growth of automatic transmissions in the '50s. Consider that in 1949 only twenty-five percent of the autos manufactured had an automatic transmission. By 1959 that number jumped to seventy-two percent.

Today, as we celebate the Fabulous '50s, an era of which people have a hard time letting go, we think of all the collector cars of that decade. Not only were the Big Three represented for those ten years, but a great many interesting independent manufacturers offered some pretty amazing cars which still look great today. Perhaps a '52 Hudson Hornet catches your eye, or maybe that handsome '53 Studebaker Starliner coupe? Or that '56 Chrysler 300 B, or maybe a '57 Ford Skyliner — read that retractable hardtop. Or was it the rare '57 Pontiac Safari station wagon, seldom seen in '57 anywhere?

Somewhere there waits for you a product of the 1950s. Perhaps it's a red convertible you never had. Perhaps it's a choice from an automobile company that's long been gone. Chances are this powerful link — a car of your dreams — will transport you back to a bygone era: the Fabulous '50s.

Fifties Fever Makes a Return Engagement

Ah, the fifties! If you're too young to remember them, at least you know all about them: Casey Stengel and Sugar Ray Robinson. Ducktails and ponytails. Captain Kangaroo and Uncle Miltie. Rock Hudson and Doris Day. The McCarthy hearings and Sputnik.

The fifties brought us the Rambler, the Corvette and the Hot Ones. Drive-in movies, hulahoops and the Mambo. Old Gold cigarettes and white bucks.

"Dragnet" and Peter Gunn. Jack Benny and Arthur Godfrey. "Ben Hur," "The Music Man" and "Gidget."

The fifties gave us chrome, fins and retractables. Conway Twitty and Neil Sedaka. Roy Rogers and Hopalong Cassidy. The fifties also gave us 3-D movies and Scrabble. Chet Huntley and David Brinkley. Jack Parr and Steve Allen. Dave Garroway and Mr. Peepers. The Mouseketeers, the Shirelles and Bill Haley and the Comets.

The fifties were all this, and more: TV quiz shows, leather jackets, flying saucers and junk food. Liberace and Floyd Patterson. "Bonanza" and "Gunsmoke."

The Thunderbird and the Chrysler 300.

The fifties also produced "From Here to Eternity" and "The Old Man and the Sea." Jack Kerouac and Allen Ginsberg. Mickey Spillane and James Baldwin. "My Fair Lady," "Porgy and Bess," and "West Side Story."

It was the fifties that gave us the polio vaccine, ignited the civil rights movement, created the space program and nurtured the minds of a King and a Kennedy.

Hobbyists who look back on the fifties nostalgically as "the good old days" can take heart. The '90s generation is rediscovering the fifties.

Today, such fifties manifestations as the Edsel and '55 Chevy are being used in magazine and TV ads to plug everything from stereo systems to women's

shoes. Men and women's clothing stores are pitching the "Fifties Look." Argyle socks, saddle shoes, Ozzie and Harriet T-shirts, angora sweaters, black denims and ankle socks are just a few of the more nostalgic items.

Barber shops and beauty salons, too, are plugging "Fifties Haircuts." Grease for the men and red nail polish for the women are usually included.

Davy Crockett hats, gumball machines and Jerry Lee Lewis records are making a comeback, according to *Time* magazine. So is the "modern" furniture that was prevalent during the fifties. Wrought-iron ashtrays, boomerang-shaped cocktail tables, bucket chairs, rocket-shaped salt and pepper shakers and garishly colored couches with spindly legs are some of the "hot" items mentioned in a recent *Rhode Island Journal* article titled "Selling the Fabulous '50s."

"Ice-cream Sodas for Two" (fifties-style, of course) is a popular feature of ice-cream parlors across the country today. Piggy banks, Dinah Shore posters and "Ike and Dick" campaign buttons are being ressurected by gift and specialty stores. Parakeets— which were the rage in pets during the fifties—are being promoted by pet shops across the nation.

The ritzy New York-based Bloomingdale's department store chain is cashing in on the fifties craze with Marilyn Monroe Boutiques in five states. The World Doll Company, too, is selling porcelain Marilyn Monroe dolls for $400.

"There can be no doubt," the *New York Times* recently editorialized, "that a fifties revival is in full swing."

"Whatever the reason," the *Times* concluded, "the fifties are making history once again." Which can only be cause for celebration among collectors of fifties cars and, for that matter, all old car nuts. Cheers.

A wild slanting fin treatment marked 1959 Buicks.

The Art of Tailfins

Rage of the 1950s

By Charles Webb

Everyone knows tailfins originated with Cadillac in 1948. But it was Chrysler's Virgil Exner who made them popular.

When the noted stylist joined the company in 1949, its cars had all the pizzazz of a discount store's cheapest refrigerator. Even Chrysler's reputation for superior engineering couldn't convince a style-conscious public to buy plain-looking cars, especially when there were so many other flashier ones from which to choose. The corporation's sales began to decline.

However, Exner was able to turn things around when his "Forward Look" 1955 models debuted. These cars were unmistakably high fashion. And their most prominent design feature was tailfins. Unlike some of the competition, the fins were integral to the car's styling, not tacked on.

Virtually every American automaker made use of fins at one time or another during the 1950s and/or 1960s, although they didn't all call them that. On some they were "twin tower taillights," "rear blades," or "stabilizers." And their sizes varied greatly. Read on and you may come across some cars you forgot even had them.

Aero-Willys

Willys had modest fins, beginning with the 1952 models. They seemed Cadillac-inspired, but lacked the standard of the world's finesse.

Buick

The first fins to appear on a Buick showed up on the 1954 models. As tailfins go, they were rather conservative, except for the bold chrome ones on the limited production Skylark. In 1955, the entire line had swept back taillights. Even then, Buicks fins were restrained and well integrated into the overall design, so much so they aren't generally thought of as "finny." Until 1958. These had the heaviest looking fins of any car that year or since.

The killer shark look was replaced by a wild slanting fin treatment in 1959. The '60s were slightly refined versions of the same. In 1963 and 1964, a slight "fin" returned. It was most noticeable on the Electra.

Cadillac

Cadillac's fin was inspired by the World War II Lockhead P-38 fighter plane. It first appeared in 1948 models, and became quite prominent by 1954. A year later, Eldorados had a new pointed fin. The original "fishtail" look disappeared entirely in 1957. Top-of-the-line Eldorados had their own sporty tailfins which gave their rear decks a chubby cheeks look. (Twenty years later, designer Ron Hill said of the fins, "They look hideous to me now, though at the time I remember I was pretty proud of that car.")

The ultimate tailfin was on the 1959 models. From

The 1959 Cadillac epitomizes the ultimate tailfin.

1960 on, Cadillac fins steadily shrank. 1964 is generally considered the last year the make used tailfins. It may be the most attractive example of that styling feature. Yet Cadillac continued the fin look for many years. It is even present in some recent models.

Chevrolet

If the fastback body style had been continued, the 1953 Chevys might have looked like they had fins. The '54s deliberately tried to create this impression. So did the '55s with their notched taillights, and a side view of the '56 reveals fin-like styling. But it wasn't until 1957 that fins arrived on Chevrolet. In '58, the make replaced fins with a sculptured rear deck treatment. However, they reappeared in their most dramatic form on Chevrolets in 1959. After the face-lifted 1960 model, they weren't used again.

Chrysler

The first Chrysler fins appeared in 1949. They were rather puny and looked added on. The make wouldn't have any fins to speak of until 1955. A year later, it received some of the best looking tailfins ever.

Chrysler's fins grew along with the rest of the car in 1957. The gently slanting versions on the 1960 looked

For Chevrolet, fins appeared in their most dramatic form on the 1959 model.

The '57 Dodge wore tasteful tailfins.

especially nice from the rear. The make got rid of its fins in 1962, although a ridge did reappear on 1964 models.

DeSoto

The '49 DeSoto had small taillights rising timidly from the rear fenders. But the make's first real tailfins arrived with the "Forward Look" in 1955. Apparently that was what the public wanted. Sales shot up from the previous year's model.

The make's fins went from mild to snazzy in '56 and grew considerably thereafter. Perhaps the most attractive use of fins came in 1960. But by then DeSotos were on their way out. Their last year was 1961, which featured unusual shark-nose fins. The 1962 models, planned before production was

stopped, were finless.

Dodge

Tiny chrome fins were placed above the taillights of 1949 Dodges. Slight fins appeared in 1953, and they were accented with chrome on top-of-the-line models in 1954. The "flair fashioned" '55 Dodges with their twin-jet taillights were the first with bold, unmistakable tailfins. The make's wildest use of swept-wing styling occurred in 1959. The next year's models were tame in comparison. By 1961, highly stylized rear body sculpturing replaced fins.

Ford

Although not famous for them, Ford may have used fins the best way to accent the car's styling. They first got them in 1955. The graceful ones used on

Ford's use of tailfins accented the car's styling. A Thunderbird is shown above.

'57 models were particularly attractive on the Thunderbird. With the exception of 1960 models, full-size Fords continued to make restrained use of tailfins through 1961. Fairlanes and T-birds had them until 1963.

Henry J

The Henry J was the first compact with fins. It kept them throughout its short life (1950-1954). Whether or not they added to the car's appeal is debatable. But they did give this rather plain, basic transportation automobile a little flair.

Hudson

Hudsons got the tailfin look in 1955. The next year, they even had little fins over the headlights. The '57 models had the largest fins, but that didn't help sales. Only 4,108 '57 Hudsons were made, and the make was discontinued in June of that year.

Imperial

Chrysler Corporation's top make came out with small fins in 1955. A couple years later they were huge. Imperial designers tried to capture the feel of the classics in 1961 models, yet that year's pointy fins detracted from their objective. The faint fins of 1962 and 1963 were far more harmonious with the rest of the car's styling. By 1964, Imperial considered fins passé.

Kaiser

The huge rear fender integrated taillights on '52 Kaisers gave them a tailfin look. The addition of chrome trim over the next few years accentuated that appearance.

Lincoln

Some people might deny 1952-'54 Mexican Road Race Lincolns had fins, but there was no doubt about the '55s. And one of the most beautifully finned cars

The canted rear blades on the '57 Lincoln looked somewhat faddish.

13

It wasn't until 1958 that a real tailfin existed for Oldsmobile.

1958 was the last model year for Packard, and it went out in "fin style."

was the '56 Lincoln. Several car buffs even like it better than the much acclaimed Continental Mark II. The canted rear blades on the face-lifted '57s looked faddish. Lincoln's fins were more restrained from 1958 to 1960. The trend-setting 1961 model introduced Continental Mark II-inspired rear deck treatment.

Mercury

Mercurys had the most attractive rear ends of any car in 1954. They were jazzed up considerably the following year. The slanted "V" shaped taillights gave the '57 to '59 Mercs a stylized fin look, but the first traditional tailfins didn't appear until 1960 on Comets and 1961 on full-size models. Small, tasteful fins remained through the 1964 model year.

Nash

Nashes never had wild fins like many other makes, yet they did make use of this style feature. Their sky flow fenders debuted in 1951 and remained (with changes) until Nash's demise in 1957.

Oldsmobile

The first Oldsmobile fins were small chrome trim pieces on the rear fenders of the 1949s. The '57 had a somewhat fin look from the side, but it wasn't until 1958 that a real fin existed. It only lasted through 1959. A distinctive yet subtle tailfin appeared in 1963 and vanished by 1965.

Packard

A bit of chrome trim on rear fenders of some 1951 to 1954 models gave Packards a tailfin look. This is especially true of '53 and '54 Caribbeans. The restyled '55 models had a definite fin except for Clippers. They didn't get them until a year later. In 1957, Packards seemed out to prove how awkward big fins looked on small cars. They succeeded in convincing most would-be customers. Packard was no more after the 1958 model year.

Plymouth

Except for the wagons, Plymouths had tiny fins in 1949. Fin-like chrome trim also appeared on the '53s and '54s. Tailfins officially arrived the next year. They blended beautifully with the new styling. Sharp-peaked tailfins came in 1956. Plymouth fins seemed to get larger and wilder every year until 1961, when they were eliminated on full-size cars. The compact Valiant continued to use fins into the mid-1960s.

According to the 1960 Plymouth sales catalog, the purpose of fins (or "stablizers" as they preferred to call them) was significant. It had to do with bringing "the center of pressure back toward the rear" of the car. Apparently wind tunnel tests at the University of Detroit found fins reduced the need to make steering corrections in cross winds by twenty percent.

Plymouth tailfins seemed to get larger and wilder every year; shown here is a 1959 Fury.

By 1958, the lovely Studebaker became an ordinary-looking "finny" car.

Pontiac

Fins came to Pontiacs in 1953, but it wasn't until 1957 the raised rear fender look gave way to a more stereotypical tailfin. That only lasted a year. Fins returned (in a different style) in 1959, vanished again, and reappeared (very low key) in 1961. They faded away by 1965.

Rambler

If you look closely, you can see why 1953-1955 Ramblers can be included among cars with tailfins. The '56 and '57 models are more obvious, and there is no debating '58 Ramblers had fins. The make toned down its fins by 1960, and two years later did away with them altogether.

Studebaker

The 1953 Studebaker was the sleekest American car available that year. It was also one of the few with tailfins. By 1957, the fins started to resemble those used on the '57 Pontiac. They were increasingly awkward and didn't seem to fit the car's over-all styling. Even the sporty Hawk was burdened with almost tacky looking fins.

By 1958, the uncommonly beautiful Studebaker styling originated five years earlier was face-lifted into an ordinary-appearing "finny" car. For 1962, designer Brook Stevens made a few refinements, which included whacking off the Hawk's fins, and Studebaker was gorgeous once again.

The Decade of Dazzle

This 1957 Corvette, owned by Ken Buttolph of Peru, Wisconsin, is one of 63 cars in Ken's current collection. This is Ken's third '57 Corvette. He also owns a '78 Corvette Indianapolis 500 pace car.

Looking much like a mid-century DeSoto dealership is this scene of restored postwar DeSotos (left to right: 1955, 1956, 1952, 1948 and 1947 models) parked in front of a '50s nostalgia club during a National DeSoto Club convention. (Courtesy Gregory J. Walters).

Terry Hoeman's 1955 Imperial two-door hardtop is an excellent example of Chrylser Corporation's completely restyled cars for 1955. Hoeman hails from Columbus, Nebraska.

Ken Block, of Cedar Rapids, Iowa, says his 1956 Chrysler 300B was a "refugee from a farmer's machine shed." Dubbed "the banker's hot rod," the 300B was an early entrant in the great horsepower race.

Donald Bodah's 1959 Impala four-door hardtop is completely restored; the engine compartment has been detailed to original, according to the Tuscola, Illinois man.

Jackson Taylor's 1958 Chevy Impala features all new chrome plating, rebuilt 283 V-8, power steering, power brakes and Powerglide transmission. According to the Green Lake, Wisconsin resident, the car was purchased from a museum.

Tom Whelan's 1959 Cadillac four-door hardtop has 49,000 original miles on the odometer, according to the Waukesha, Wisconsin resident.

This 1950 Oldsmobile 88 convertible, belonging to Lars Anderson of Oconomowoc, Wisconsin, was recovered from the slums of Cincinnati. It received a frame-off restoration and is now used for recreational travel.

Lawrence G. Freund's 1955 Pontiac Star Chief convertible is a major award winner for the McHenry, Illinois resident. Freund purchased the car in 1980 in Indiana, where it had been stored in a shed.

Ralph Marolf's 1959 Ford two-door hardtop has an original interior and is loaded with options. Less than 40,000 miles are on the odometer, the Farley, Iowa man says.

Wayne Holous' 1951 Mercury two-door Sports Coupe is a good example of the third year of the '49-'50-'51 era popularized by James Dean. 1951 was also the third and final year of the all-new body style introduced by Mercury in 1949.

Robert E. Riley's two Thunderbirds, a yellow '55 and a pink '56, illustrate the high-spiritedness of the early T-birds. In fact, the Madison, Wisconsin man's yellow T-bird was featured as the "poster car" for the 1992 Iola Old Car Show, which spotlighted cars from the 1950s.

Dennis and Paula Hardison's 1955 Mercury Montclair Sun Valley has a Plexiglas roof. According to the Lindenhurst, Illinois man, the car was restored five years ago.

Hudson's top-of-the-line series for 1950 was the Commodore, which came with either six (502) or eight (504) cylinders. Pictured here is a 1950 Hudson Commodore 502.

Although Kaiser's passenger car business was on the decline in 1953, some refreshing design changes marked that year's models. Note the chrome strip used on the tops of the rear fenders to create miniature tailfins. This is a 1953 Kaiser Dragon.

This 1955 Packard 400 two-door hardtop belongs to Mike Truex of Pontiac, Michigan. 1955 was a year of innovations for Packard. The company introduced its first modern V-8 as well as self-leveling torsion bar suspension and push-button transmission.

1955

Year of the New Car

By R. Perry Zavitz

The cost of car ownership is only $598 per year. Gasoline, oil, tires, and maintenance cost only 3½ cents per mile. That was the claim of the Automobile Club of Michigan in 1955.

Let us look back almost forty years to see what the new cars were like, the cars that gave that kind of performance in terms of money.

The 1955 model year was one of the most exciting and significant in all car history for the United States. Many new styles were introduced, and lots of new V-8 engines were also featured.

By 1955 only two minor makes did not have a modern V-8 to offer, at least optionally. (Kaiser and Willys enthusiasts will strongly object to that word "minor" but it is used simply because those two cars did not survive 1955.)

Oct. 22, 1954 was the introduction date of the Ford Thunderbird. With its high-profile pre-introduction promotion, there was little surprise when the Thunderbird reached showrooms. Its acceptance was widespread and has remained so even today as a collector car. The base price was $2,944.

Other 1955 Ford models were not introduced until three weeks later. The completely restyled Fords came in three series as before, but Fairlane was the new name for the top line. Crown Victoria was a new body type in that series. Often referred to as a hardtop, it technically was not because of the wide chrome band that crossed over the roof at the mid point and went down to the beltline. For an extra $70 a transparent front roof section could be had. The Crown Victoria with the see-through roof was a continuation

The first 1955 Ford to be introduced was the very popular Thunderbird. Those famous two-seater models are still very popular.

Pontiac's new V-8 replaced both the flathead six and straight-eight engines of the past. New styling was another feature for 1955.

The completely restyled 1955 Plymouth was the longest in its price class.

of the 1954 Skyliner.

Ford's ohv V-8, new for 1954, was expanded from 239.4 cubic inches to 272 cid. Power consequently rose from 130 hp to 162 hp or 182 hp with an optional power package.

One week after Ford's introduction, Pontiac showrooms were crowded by people curious to see Pontiac's totally new styling and engine. There were 109 new body, engine, and chassis changes claimed. Except for the double silver streaks on the hood, Pontiac's new styling was totally different from its former appearance. Along with the new styling came two new model names. The two lower-priced series were dubbed 860 and 870. The Star Chief remained the name of Pontiac's top line.

Pontiac was the second last straight-eight holdout. But its memorable 268 cid 122 hp motor was replaced by a modern 287 cid 180 hp V-8. In fact, that V-8 also replaced Pontiac's flathead six.

The use of new-design V-8s was not restricted to Ford in the low-priced field. Plymouth, when its Nov. 17 debut for 1955 took place, offered a variety of V-8 engines along with brand new styling. The flathead six was standard, but a modern V-8 of 260 cubic inches was offered in either 167 hp or, with a power package, 177 hp. An even smaller 241 cid V-8 was also available, and it produced 157 hp.

The completely restyled 1955 Plymouth was the longest in its price class. The ten-inch growth from the 1954 models necessitated a sixty-seven-foot extension of Plymouth's main assembly line in Detroit.

One day after Plymouth's introduction, Cadillac presented its 1955 models. Styling was a revision of the new-for-1954 design. The Eldorado, the only survivor of GM's super luxury convertibles introduced for 1953, took on a more distinctive appearance with rear fins unlike those of the other Cadillacs. Those fins, it turned out, were a forecast of the fins on the regular Cadillac three years hence.

Although displacement remained the same as before, Cadillac engine output was raised from 230 hp to 250 hp, in part by increasing compression to 9.0:1 — the highest for 1955. The Eldorado, however, had a 270 hp rating. That was the highest rating, but only for two months.

Buick and Oldsmobile made their official 1955 appearances on Nov. 19, 1954. Like Cadillac, their styling was a refinement of the new 1954 bodies. Also like Cadillac, power was increased from the same displacement. For Buick, the 264 cid V-8 of the Special series was rerated at 188 hp — up from 143 (or 150

The Cadillac Eldorado sprouted its own tailfins. These 1955 fins were much like those on other Cadillacs in 1958.

Buick Riviera four-door models were offered only in the Special and Century series for 1955. Oldsmobile also offered four-door hardtops in 1955.

with Dynaflow) in the 1954 models. The 322 V-8 had a 236 hp rating regardless of series or transmission. Previously it had four ratings ranging from 177 hp to 200 hp.

Olds raised its output from 170 hp in the 88 to 185 hp. The Super 88 and 98 models were powered by a 202 hp version of the same engine.

With a total of 260,608 Buicks and an estimated 144,000 Oldsmobile hardtops built, these two cars were the undisputed leaders in hardtop production during 1954. That leadership was dramatically underscored when production of four-door hardtops began in March 1955. The 1949-'50 Kaiser Virginian and 1951 Frazer Manhattan, which were produced in small quantities, really introduced the four-door hardtop look, but it was actually Buick and Olds that made such models popular.

Buick Riviera four-door models were offered only in the Special and Century series for 1955. Olds four-door Holidays were available in all three series. Together Buick and Oldsmobile built over 240,000 four-door hardtops during 1955, with Buick having a slight edge over Olds in total production. That was a tremendous vote of confidence for a new body type. Prices ranged from $71 to $211 more than comparable four-door sedans.

Lincoln, which inaugurated its 1955 model year on Nov. 23, 1954, had only cursory styling changes. An enlarged and more powerful engine was its main feature. A one-eighth-inch greater cylinder bore increased the displacement from 317 to 341 cubic inches. That made the Lincoln motor larger than Cadillac's. Horsepower was raised from 205 to 225, which was 25 less than Cadillac's rating. A new Turbo-Drive transmission was standard, and it replaced the bought-from-GM HydraMatic Lincoln had been relying on for several years.

To Lincoln should go the gizmo-of-the-year award. Its optional Multi-Luber appeared only as a small button on the dash. When it was activated, the chassis wass instantly lubricated at eleven different points for that "just lubricated ride." Lincoln's Cosmopolitan name was replaced by Custom. Capri continued as the top line.

When Mercury made its appearance on Dec. 2, 1954, a new top line, the Montclair, was offered. Fresh new styling featured a double bar bumper, which also served as the grille. Behind it was an engine with expanded bore and stroke. The new 292 cid V-8 developed 188 hp to 198 hp. The latter was standard in Merc-O-Matic-equipped Monclairs. The Sun Valley glass top model was a member of the Montclair series.

Studebaker led the 1955 parade of new cars on Oct. 6, 1954, but it was not until Jan. 10, 1955 that the Speedster model made its debut. The former top

When Mercury made its appearance on Dec. 2, 1954, a new top line, the Montclair, was offered.

The Studebaker Speedster had a new 185 hp V-8 engine and special leather interior. It was perhaps a forerunner of the Golden Hawk, which followed in 1956.

line Land Cruiser sedan was expanded into a full-fledged series of sedan, coupe, and hardtop for 1955. A new name, actually a used name, was uncovered, and the top series became the President line.

The former 120 hp 232.6 cid V-8 was discarded. It was replaced by a very small 224.3 cid V-8, but it developed 140 hp. That was used in the Commander models until January, when the President V-8 replaced it. It had a displacement of 259.2 cubic inches. The Commander developed 162 hp, but in the President the output was an advertised 185 hp.

It was this 185-hp engine that the Speedster used. Basically the Speedster was like the other Studebaker hardtops of 1955 — with a vast wasteland of chrome on the front end. However, there were detail differences on the exterior and a distinctive leather interior, which made the Speedster something special. The Speedster heralded the famed Golden Hawk of 1956.

Studebaker's new partner, Packard, was the most persistent straight-eighter, outlasting Pontiac by a few weeks. However, for 1955 it succumbed to the popular V-8 trend. An overhead valve, high (8.5:1) compression, over-square V-8 in two sizes replaced the three big flathead straight-eights of 1954. The 320 cid version developed 225 hp. The larger 352 cid engine, which was the industry's largest for 1955, developed 245, 260 and 275 hp, depending on model.

Extensive revisions to the 1954 bodies gave Packard a very new look for 1955. The Clipper name was revived, and, in fact, the junior models were not officially Packards, but Clippers — a point the public preferred to ignore. They were all considered to be Packards.

The Caribbean carried on by using the new styling and new V-8. With the 352-cid 275-hp engine, the Caribbean could brag that it had the industry's biggest and most powerful engine available — most powerful only for the time being, though.

It was on Oct. 28, 1954 when Chevrolet introduced its 1955 models, but not until the following Jan. 26 that the line was completed. Brand new styling was the most obvious feature of the 1955 Chevrolets, but the new optional V-8 was at least as important as the

The Packard Patrician was the top sedan for 1955. The body was reworked, but the V-8 engine was new. It had the largest displacement of the 1955 cars.

Brand new styling for the 1955 Chevrolet was highlighted by the late arriving Nomad. The new V-8 engine was a popular option that year.

car's outward appearance. The 265 cid V-8 developed 162 hp in standard form. A power-pack was available for those wanting 180 hp. In the Corvette, for which styling was not changed for 1955, the optional V-8 was a 195-hp version. Along with the Corvette's introduction for 1955 came a $724 price cut for the six. Even the V-8 Corvette was $589 less than the previous year's six.

Together with the 1955 Corvette, Chevrolet's new Nomad station wagon was launched. As one of the most stylish wagons ever mass-produced, there is little wonder that it is one of the most sought-after of Chevrolet's extremely popular mid-'50s models. Pontiac got on the Nomad bandwagon with its version, the Safari.

Like Chevrolet and Pontiac, the 1955 Dodge, DeSoto, and Chrysler models were introduced in the fall of 1954. Each offered fresh new styling in sharp contrast to previous staid styling. But for 1955, not only was their styling much more attractive, but all the V-8 models were given a full dose of pep pills.

The Dodge V-8 was enlarged to 270 cubic inches from 241, and output raised from 150 hp to 175 hp.

DeSoto abandoned its six-cylinder models for V-8 power across the board. A 291-cid engine — increased from 276 cid — powered all DeSotos with 185 hp. With the demise of the DeSoto six, the Powermaster series went into oblivion. The Firedome remained, but a new top line, the Fireflite series, was added.

Chrysler also dropped its six when it stuck a 301 cid V-8 in the Windsor DeLuxe line. It developed 188 hp — just nominally more than DeSoto. The New Yorker DeLuxe (there was no standard New Yorker for 1955) and Imperials retained the 331-cid V-8, but raised the power to 250 hp like Cadillac.

Chrysler's *piece de resistance* came on Feb. 10, 1955 with the introduction of a new model called the 300. The name was inspired by its power. Three hundred horsepower was developed from its engine. That overshadowed the Caribbean's 275 hp, but Packard's 352 cubes remained the largest displacement for the model year.

The Chrysler 300 was a composite of different Chrysler body components. Basically, it was a Chrysler two-door hardtop with the big, bold Imperial grille. The interior was leather. Wherever the 300 was raced, it made headlines, winning 37 major races during the year.

American Motors' Rambler wore two hats for 1955 — two medallions actually — Nash or Hudson. Criss-cross grillework was about the only styling change made to Rambler for the new season.

The senior Nash and Hudson models were the last of the 1955s to appear. The Nash, which went on display Feb. 17, had revised styling and an optional V-8 engine for the Ambassador. It was Nash's first V-8 ever and its first postwar eight. The new engine was Packard's 320 cid motor, which somehow lost some of its potency in the transplant. It developed 208 hp in Nash, down significantly from 225 in Packard.

The Nash-Healey, sadly, became a car of the past, as did Hudson's Italia in 1954. The Wasp and Hornet were the only previous Hudson lines to survive the 1954 merger. But there was a degree of regret regarding them. Although they had totally new styling for the first time since 1948, that styling was actually a thinly disguised Nash. More Hudson identity was evident under the hood, however. The Wasp used the 202 cid six-cylinder engine of the now defunct Jet. With dual carburetors, this engine developed an acceptably modest 115 hp. The 1955 Hornet six used Hudson's famous 308 cid engine. It developed 160 hp in standard form or 170 hp with two carburetors. A Hornet option was the 208 hp Packard V-8.

Kaiser, which had been hanging by a thread through 1954, announced its practically unchanged 1955 models on Jan. 6, 1955. On Jan. 20, it cut that thread when it announced that it would move out of the United States and set up production in Argentina. The only Kaisers built during 1955 were produced in May and June, but they were exported to Argentina.

Willys, Kaiser's runningmate, fared a bit better. The greatest change since the car's introduction was made to the grille for 1955. The Ace name was no longer used. Two- and four-door Custom models were

The last shall be first! The last 1955 model to be introduced was the Chrysler 300. Its 300 horsepower helped it win 37 major races that year.

Top: Willys passenger car production ended in April 1955. Bottom: Kaiser also quit making cars in 1955 and moved to South America to set up a factory.

available as well as a pleasant-looking hardtop, the Bermuda. Production of Willys passenger cars ended in Toledo in April 1955. Willys Jeep-type station wagons continued, however.

Despite the withdrawal of Kaiser and Willys from the American market, 1955 was a tremendous year. Every other make of car enjoyed improved sales during the year, with two exceptions: The little-changed Lincoln had a registration drop of 3½ percent, and Studebaker registrations were down a mere 153 units. The industry as a whole chalked up a total of 7,169,908 new car registrations during 1955, setting a new record which was not broken until 1963.

While we're looking back, let's focus on what some people expected the future would hold for the auto industry.

Early in 1955, *Fortune* magazine's editor predicted that new car sales would average close to $5 billion a year over the 1955-'59 period. The actual average turned out to be almost $6 billion in spite of the recession of 1958.

The Bureau of Public Roads predicted that the total registration of 61.3 million motor vehicles in 1955 would rise to 81 million during the next decade. That prediction missed the mark by about ten percent. The Department of Commerce listed the U.S. total vehicle registrations for 1965 at just over 89 million.

A Cornell Medical College car crash researcher predicted that in ten years cars would have maximum safety features. That did not come about in the time frame expected, but the flurry and scurry concerning safety features was becoming evident in showrooms about a decade later.

In May 1955, L.L. "Tex" Colbert, Chrysler Corporation president, said that by 1975 the "one-car family could be in the minority and many families may be using three and four cars."

GMC Truck and Coach Division General Manager P.J. Monaghan said that truck sales would triple in twenty years. New truck registrations in 1955 amounted to 957,000. In 1975 the total was 2,397,400, which was only about 2½ times the '55 sum.

The chief body engineer at Chrysler said that by 1980 family cars would be of three types: 1) electronically guided highway cruisers for long distance travel, 2) urbanite cars for intra-city runs, and 3) sports cars for "good old-fashioned driving fun."

The dean of the College of Engineering at the University of Michigan predicted that by the year 2000, electric cars would return. They would receive their power from overhead lines connected to central atomic power stations. We'll see!

Chrysler in the Fifties

They Built Dreams for the Masses

By John Lee

Given the staid, utilitarian boxes on wheels as 1950 dawned, who would have imagined we'd be driving dream cars by the end of the decade?

Huge expanses of glass, automatic transmissions activated by push-buttons, seats that pivoted outward to ease entry and exit, stabilizing tailfins — this was the stuff of the "cars of the future" envisioned on the covers of *Popular Science* and *Mechanix Illustrated*. By 1960 Chrysler Corp. would have incorporated these features and more.

The decade of the fifties saw Chrysler abandon its traditional styling conservatism to lead the way though a brief period of finned flamboyance, color and pizzazz.

Virgil Exner was the architect. Joining the Chrysler design staff in 1949 and rising to head that department by mid-decade, he was responsible for designing idea cars which Ghia of Italy turned into functional models. Creations like the K-310, Adventurer and Cabana prepared the public for such production innovations as free-standing taillights and spare tire covers embossed onto the deck lid.

"The Hundred-Million Dollar Look" of 1955 referred to what the corporation spent to totally redesign the entire line: Plymouth, Dodge, DeSoto, Chrysler and — designated a separate make for the first time — Imperial. It was a gamble that paid off with record sales and made Chrysler the company to watch for styling trends. Another total restyle two years later popularized tailfins and wedge shapes that would characterize the line through the end of the decade.

While styling provided visibility and showroom appeal, Chrysler didn't neglect the engineering that had built its reputation from the beginning. The company's first V-8 engine, introduced in the 1951 Chrysler, over the next few years replaced the reliable, but dated, L-head sixes and eights. In typical Chrysler fashion, it was over-engineered with hemispherical combustion chambers that could take advantage of the coming higher octane gasoline. Churning out 180 horsepower, it topped Cadillac by 20 horsepower from the same displacement, thus setting off the horsepower race.

V-8 power was phased into the rest of the corporate line — DeSoto in 1952, Dodge in 1953 and Plymouth in 1955. By the end of the decade, lighter, less-expensive wedge combustion chamber V-8s had succeeded the hemis, and a modern, overhead valve "slant six" that would make its mark in economy and longevity had been introduced. Chrysler engineering also developed and tested gas turbine engines.

Power steering in 1951, push-button automatic transmission controls and record players in 1956 and torsion bar front suspension in 1957 were other Chrysler engineering successes.

Although none of the prototye sports car designs became reality, the high-powered, limited production Chrysler 300 series introduced in 1955 paved the way for personal-luxury models to follow.

From fins to top-speed figures, Chrysler Corp. truly achieved new heights during the exciting decade of the fifties!

Chrysler

As the accompanying ad from a '50s magazine shows, wood was seen as a material with "enduring distinction" then. The wood-body Chrysler Town & Country Series was continued into 1950 as this hardtop-styled Newport model.

A Chrysler engineering advance for 1951 — the introduction of the "Firepower" hemi V-8 — was honored by Indianapolis Motor Speedway in selecting a New Yorker convertible to pace the Indy 500.

The 4,000 convertibles made by Chrysler in 1951 represented 2.8 percent of total industry sales. This 1951 Windsor ragtop looks right at home in this setting of "postwar prosperity."

After World War II, the U.S. Government's Economic Stablization Agency was called upon to help smooth the transition from a wartime to peacetime economy. The OPS (Office of Price Stabilization) froze automobile prices at the Dec. 1, 1950 level until March 1, 1951. After that, price hikes could be authorized by OPS on an individual basis. On May 28, Chrysler was permitted an increase of $251.19 on its luxury-class Imperials, which included this 1951 convertible.

The custom auto body industry declined drastically after World War II. One old-line firm — Derham of Rosemont, Pennsylvania — kept its doors open building cars like this 1952 Chrysler parade phaeton. Three such cars were constructed — one for New York City, one for Detroit and one for Los Angeles. All three cars were restyled in the mid-1950s and all three survive today.

Power steering and power brakes were automobile options that came into popular acceptance in the early '50s. Both were offered on this stunning 1952 Chrysler New Yorker convertible.

In 1952, the postwar *Office of Price Stabilization* gave Chrysler another "hardship case" price adjustment. When it went into effect on Feb. 11, this 1952 Imperial sedan became more expensive. No one would know from this photo reflecting status and wealth that Chrysler was having economic problems.

In the '50s, vacationing became the great American pastime. World War II had shown a once provincial-minded society how the rest of the world looked. In automobile-land, the stylish postwar hardtops were often named after popular vacation spots — Riviera, Bel Air, Catalina. Oldsmobile opted for the name Holiday, while Chrysler products, such as this 1953 Imperial, used the term "Newport" (as in Newport, Rhode Island) to designate pillarless coupes.

With the recession of 1953-1954 impacting sales and limiting product development investments, Chrysler designers made creative use of what they had to work with. This 1953 Chrysler New Yorker club coupe got a hardtop-like rear wraparound window, although it's a pillared two-door sedan.

Long skirts and cropped jackets with semi-fitted waistlines were fashionable for the ladies in 1953. Hats and "Audrey Hepburn" haircuts were also trendy. Pointy shoes, cut low to the soles on both sides, rounded out a perfect ensemble. In contrast to such up-to-date clothing designs, the boxy 1953 Chrysler New Yorker sedan looked stately but stodgy.

The reclusive millionaire Howard Hughes made the tabloids throughout the early '50s, often with Hollywood star-lets on his arms. This 1954 Chrysler New Yorker, made especially for Hughes, had a one-of-a-kind air filtration system.

Wealthier Americans making long journeys in 1954 were likely to ride passenger trains like "The Canadian" — or even fly. Which probably explains Chrysler's low sales of station wagons. It was the only company offering this body style in the "high-priced field" that season. This is a 1954 Windsor Town & Country wagon.

The modern (for 1955) house behind this Chrysler Windsor Newport coupe probably had an Amana air conditioning system, such as that shown in the accompanying 1957 advertisement. About 15,000 central home air-conditioning systems were sold in 1955, twice as many as the year before.

To enter the youth market in 1955, Chrysler executive Bob Rodgers created the limited edition "300" Letter car. The hemi-powered hardtop with an Imperial grille tore up America's stock car racing tracks with ace drivers like Frank "Rebel" Mundy behind the wheel.

"The Beave" (or a look-alike) sitting on the steps doesn't look too happy about Mom and Pop's new 1955 Chrysler Windsor station wagon. Actually, "Leave It To Beaver" wasn't on TV screens yet — but comedian Phil Silvers was popularizing the new medium with his "Sergent Bilko" character.

The 350th anniversary of Rembrandt's birth was celebrated by the international art world in 1956. Major artistic developments in the United States included the Whitney's Annual Survey of Contemporary American Art and a "Recent Drawings U.S.A." exhibition at the Museum of Modern Art. Reflecting the artistic talents of stylist Virgil Exner was Chrysler's new "Forward Look," seen here on a Windsor convertible and New Yorker four-door sedan.

In 1957, the average American production worker put in 39.2 hours per week and earned $82.32. With a price tag of $4,838, this new Imperial Southampton four-door cost more than the average man made in a year.

Women's hats were worn off the face in 1957, straight if cloches or swaggers, side-tilted if berets or turbans. Short jackets and long skirts were the rage. This stylish woman is driving a Chrysler New Yorker four-door hardtop.

In 1957, Indiana passed legislation requiring drivers to pass an examination every few years, including vision and written tests; created a Division of School Traffic Safety Education; made all licenses for those under 18 years old probationary; and increased insurance requirements. This 1957 Chrysler 300C was "Back Home in Indiana" for a club meet at the Indianapolis Motor Speedway.

During 1958, America suffered its most severe recession since World War II. The Gross National Product dropped by $6 billion, and 5,437,000 people were out of work. It was not a good year to be selling cars such as this Crown Imperial limousine.

Country club living was the dream of many Americans in the "Fabulous '50s." And what better "Land Yacht" was there to be seen in than an 1958 Imperial convertible?

One difference between the 1950s and today is that 40 years ago autoworkers were very loyal to the product line of the company they worked for. Notice that all the cars in the factory lot behind this 1958 Imperial Southampton sedan are Chrysler Corporation products.

Production of chromium ore (chromite) decreased from 4.7 million tons in 1957 to 3.7 million tons in 1958. The side trim on this 1958 Chrysler New Yorker convertible does little to explain this decline.

On Jan. 1, 1959, President Fulgencio Batista of Cuba fled to the Dominican Republic and Dr. Fidel Castro's rebel troops marched into Havana. During the same month, the 1959 Chrysler 300E was introduced. This limited-edition high-performance model was annually brought out just before the Chicago Automobile Show.

Architectural advances of 1959 included the completion of Frank Lloyd Wright's Beth Sholoon Synagogue in Pennsylvania and the Kaiser geodesic dome at the American exhibition in Moscow. Chrysler turned to more traditional structures to backdrop publicity photos of the year's Crown Imperial Southampton coupe. Unfortunately, even this couldn't tune down the car's wild looks sufficiently to please its conservative class of wealthy buyers.

Anyone wanting to make the U.S. Government's 1959 "Buy American" policy successful could invest in this truly as-big-as Texas 1959 Crown Imperial that had capitalism written all over its tooth grille. The new program was a reaction to fears the U.S. dollar would have to be devalued to offset the effect of a new economic problem known as "inflation."

DeSoto

DeSotos accounted for only 1.8 percent of new-car registrations in 1950. In the early '50s, an industry trade journal suggested that 200,000 cars — such as this 1950 DeSoto four-door sedan — might be made annually when the postwar economy settled down "and guns and butter no longer dictate car production." That was typical of American industry's rosy view at the start of the decade. DeSoto, however, lost ground in the 1950s sales race and disappeared in 1961.

DeSoto sales made a rare jump in 1951 when this Custom four-door sedan was sold. Nationally, the brand accounted for 2.2 percent of new-car registrations that season. An important phase of the company's business was production of taxicabs, many of which were used in New York City. In that region, DeSoto held 3.2 percent of the market.

A mid-year steel strike and Korean War government controls put a lid on DeSoto's 1952 output, which fell 19 percent. Even the up-to-date looking Sportsman Custom two-door hardtop couldn't help. Year 1952 was also the first in which DeSoto offered its 160 hp Firedome V-8, power steering, power brakes and Fluid-Torque Drive transmission.

DeSoto contributed to America's post-World War II industrial technology by opening up a new "push-button" engine plant for 1952 production. It contributed to the company's ability to produce 60 bodies and engines per hour that year. One model offered in 1953 was the V-8 powered Firedome station wagon.

When a steel strike closed the DeSoto factory in 1952, the company tried to take advantage of the slowdown by staging a secretive, though dramatic, "dress rehearsal" of its all-new '53 models. This 1953 DeSoto Firedome two-door hardtop prototype was described as being "a sweeping departure from the past."

Between 1950 and 1955, the population of the United States increased by 15.6 million people — a rise of about 10 percent. Maybe DeSoto felt building cars that held more people was a way to take advantage of the "baby boom." What other reason could there have been for offering this 1953 Firedome eight-passenger sedan of which only 200 examples were sold?

DeSotos were far from America's best-loved postwar automobiles, but these students from Stout University's "Old Car Club" still love the 1954 DeSoto Sportsman hardtop, which they restored as a group project. The college, in Menomonie, Wisconsin, is one of few nationwide to offer this type of extra curricular activity.

A continued trend towards increased Democratic political strength was reflected in the 1954 Congressional elections. The perfect car for taking lots of people to the polls to help support your favorite party with their votes was the 1954 DeSoto Powermaster Six station wagon.

Televisions were getting bigger in the mid-'50s, as you can see by the accompanying ad for DuMont Laboratories' 30-inch "Royal Sovereign Teleset." Also growing larger in 1955 was the DeSoto from Chrysler Corporation. This Fireflite four-door sedan stretched 217 inches bumper-to-bumper versus just over 215 inches the year before.

Limited production automobiles characterized a mid-1950s reaction to early postwar social homogenization. The 1956 DeSoto Sportsman SeVille hardtop, with its distinctive two-tone paint combinations and flashy gold wheel covers, was one of many such "Fab Fifties" models.

W. L. Rogers, of the United States Auto Club's technical committee, rode in this 1956 DeSoto Fireflite hardtop during official Indy 500 functions surrounding the 1956 race. Pat Flaherty won the 500-mile "Memorial Day Classic" with an average speed of 206.740 kilometers per mile (128.490 mph). Double-breasted men's suits — promoted as "The London Look" — saw a revival of popularity in the late 1950s.

This photo of a 1956 DeSoto Fireflite convertible pacing the Indy 500 on May 30, 1956 clearly shows why the Indianapolis Motor Speedway came to be nicknamed "The Brickyard." In later years, as race cars grew faster, more and more of the track surface was paved smooth. Today, only a small section of brick remains to commemorate the speedway's long history. (Courtesy IMSC)

American businessmen had a successful year during 1956 with the McGraw-Hill Business Week Index winding up at 154.8 percent of the 1947-'49 average and 7.1 percent higher than 1955. This DeSoto dealer seems to be enjoying his share of the upturn in demand for sales and service.

During 1956, more than 1,100,000 permanent (non-farm) homes were under construction. This brick and flagstone ranch looks fairly new. Featuring DeSoto's new grille and side trim appearance is a 1956 Firedome SeVille two-door hardtop.

Could she be reading a photocopy? The development of this new type of duplicating machine was certainly one of the major advances of the '50s for the average American. First versions were marketed in 1955, but the A.B. Dick Model 112 shown dates from 1957. Also a 1957 model is the DeSoto Adventurer two-door hardtop with optional quad headlamps (not legal in all states at the time).

Multi-car families — needing multi-car garages — were becoming much more common during the '50s. The 270 hp 1957 DeSoto Firedome Sportsman hardtop (with "Flightsweep" styling) was not exactly a family car, but the concept of different models for different purposes was part of the multi-car marketing thrust.

Cloth coats were considered very fashionable for American women in 1958. The typical lady's suit had a soft collar and slightly V-shaped neckline, with straight, buttoned closures. Straw hats, often with flower-laden brims, were popular, too. The year's fashionable transportation modes included this 1958 DeSoto Fireflite Sportsman hardtop coupe.

The accompanying ad shows a Lawn-Boy 21-inch "Automower" that matches the era of this 1958 DeSoto Firesweep Explorer station wagon. Perhaps this type of lawn mower was used to trim the grass showing behind the car. As you can see, the Lawn-Boy product of that year had a functional appearance in contrast to the DeSoto's "designer" look.

Women's clothing designers abandoned the chemise and trapeze dress styles in 1958, and withdrew to a classical look for 1959. Popular attire ran towards loose-bodiced dresses, and this model is definitely up on the latest styles. Automobile fashions didn't change quite so rapidly, with most major face-lifts following a three-year cycle. Therefore, this 1959 DeSoto Firedome Sportsman four-door hardtop continues the basic body lines introduced in 1957, with cosmetic and trim updates.

An American's average hourly earnings reached $2.21 in 1959, while average weekly earnings stood at $91.53. Both were new highs. Workers in the country were wealthier than ever before. Perhaps this explains the "rich" looks bestowed on the 1959 DeSoto Fireflite four-door Sportsman hardtop.

Dodge

These two women, fashionably dressed in 1950s cold weather attire, might be dreaming of a vacation in Miami, Florida with a visit to the city's "Spring Festival" (promoted by the inset advertisement) as part of the trip. The 1950 Dodge Custom Coronet four-door sedan was well-known for its comfortable and trouble-free road travel traits.

Golfing attire, circa 1950, included saddle shoes and bobby socks for women and cuffed pants and two-tone shoes for men. The Dodge Wayfarer convertible was perfect for weekend drives to the golf course.

Everyone seemed to enjoy "personalizing" their cars after World War II, and the auto accessories marketplace boomed. James Gwaltney, of Anderson, Ind., has dressed up his 1951 Dodge four-door sedan with everything from factory-offered extras to aftermarket goodies. How many accessories can you count in this photo?

A boom in new home construction took place as the postwar economy stabilized in the early '50s. With GI Bill benefits from wartime service, many Americans were able to purchase their dream homes. This woman seems to be day-dreaming about her 1951 Dodge Coronet sedan. Or perhaps she just doesn't know how to shift a semi-automatic transmission!

American values changed following World War II as the "good life" promised the nation's citizens higher paychecks for shorter work weeks. Some of the trappings that went with the growing perception of unbridled opportunity included water skis, a cabin cruiser and a convertible. In this case the ragtop is a 1952 Dodge Coronet.

During 1953, Dodge was one of three companies out of sixteen major truck producers to build models in all seven gross-vehicle-weight classes recognized by the industry. Seen here is a half-ton panel truck built that year.

After a quarter century of relatively constrained living and dressing, America's postwar "economy of plenty" made fashion a big focus in the United States. Cothing trends often included light pastel colors. And it wasn't long before cars began adopting pastel finishes, too. This 1953 Dodge Coronet four-door sedan sports such colors in a two-tone combination.

California was one of America's fastest growing states in the '50s. Between 1940 and 1950, its population grew from 6,907,387 to 10,586,223. By 1956, the number would be 13,433,000. Well-suited to transport growing families in the state was this 1953 Dodge Meadowbrook two-door station wagon.

Panel trucks were popular with small businessmen in the '50s. They were well-suited for delivering goods such as the DuMont Belvidere 21-inch television shown in inset ad. This 1954 Dodge Town Panel is V-8 powered judging by the hood emblem.

The rural population of the United States was declining about two percent per year in the mid-1950s. Across the country, farms and horse ranches were being turned into tract housing developments or shopping centers. Providing excellent transportation for weekend excursions into the country was the V-8-powered 1954 Dodge Royal four-door sedan.

In 1954, approximately $11.5 million worth of new dwelling units were constructed in the United States. The modern home behind the 1954 Dodge Royal sedan may have been one of them. Hats were definitely part of any smart wardrobe thirty-eight years ago, but this fellow's high crown type of hat would fall from favor by 1955, partly due to the lower heights of automobiles.

A 1954 Dodge Royal convertible with special finish and trim served as the official pace car for the Indy 500 on May 31, 1954. Race driver Bill Vukovich took the checkered flag, for the second year in a row, with an average speed of 130.840 mph — the highest ever.

Little by little, postwar trucks started adopting styling features introduced earlier on cars. This 1954 Dodge Town-Panel sports a new-for-the-year one-piece windshield. Check out the early 1930s sedan in the Chrysler factory parking lot. A good number of such cars were still in everyday use in the mid-'50s.

"You ain't nothing but a hounddog," Elvis Presley wailed on his 1956 rock 'n' roll platter. This well-dressed woman seems to be contemplating her chances of getting her upscale hounddog to climb in her 1955 Dodge Royal Lancer two-door hardtop.

Unlike cars, trucks of the early 1950s did not show major annual styling changes. This 1955 Dodge Town Wagon has two-door station wagon styling.

These women seem to be heading on a shopping spree in their 1955 Dodge Coronet Six four-door sedan. The '50s saw a spectular rise of food chains, variety stores and buying cooperatives. During 1955, the first enclosed shopping mall opened in Appleton, Wis.

Beatings prove they're unbeatable—
GOODYEAR'S NEW 3-T NYLON CORD TIRES!

NEW 3-T NYLON CUSTOM SUPER-CUSHION

GOOD/YEAR

All-new Goodyear 3-T nylon cord tires were used as original equipment on some Chrysler Corporation cars in 1956. This four-door hardtop — a new model that year — was offered in the Dodge Custom Royal Lancer line.

Fishing grew in popularity after World War II as Americans found themselves with more leisure time. In 1957, the Dingell-Johnson sport fisheries restoration program was launched and carried out in 139 different state projects. There's nothing "fishy" about the good looks of the 1957 Dodge Custom Royal Lancer two-door hardtop these anglers drove on their vacation.

With two-tone finish, whitewall tires and chrome trim, this 1957 Dodge D-100 Town Wagon looks a lot more modern, although its basic styling dates back several years. As you can see, agriculture was strong in 1957, with production holding at 1956's record levels. Farm acreage was the smallest ever, but yield per acre was the highest ever!

"Sweptwing" is used to describe this 1958 Dodge Coronet club sedan. The reference to "wings" reflects the growth of interest in aviation. On Dec. 12, 1957, Major Adrian Drew set a new world speed record for manned aircraft when he flew his U.S. Air Force "Voodoo" fighter-bomber 1,207.6 mph.

CARTER CARPAC ALL-PURPOSE CARRIER
Full length Station Wagon model shown below

A Distinctive Cartop Carrier You Will Be Proud To Own
Designed not only for carrying capacity but also to enhance the looks of your automobile. CarPac's beautifully varnished wood and sparkling hardware add "Town & Country" look. Models from $49.50 (Utility Sedan) to $125 (Full Length Station Wagon). Professional Photographer's Platform model CarPac $225. Write for folder showing all models including covers. DEALERS: We invite your inquiry. CARTER MFG. CO., 1233 S. E. Division Street, Portland, Oregon

Part car, part truck and part bus, the station wagon was perfectly suited to America's postwar mobility and suburban lifestyle. Inset ad shows one of many accessories available in the '50s for models like this 1958 Dodge Custom four-door station wagon.

While the recreational vehicle (RV) industry would really start taking off in the mid-'60s, this lifestyle trend began developing during the fabulous '50s. This double-decker camper unit on a 1958 Sweptside pickup looks more functional than stylish.

Architectural trends reflected in this 1958 photo include the wider use of enriched or decorative surfaces that added warmth and interest to the plain severity of "modern" homes. The new Dodge Town Panel FTD florist delivery truck also has many decorative options such as deluxe chrome trim and two-tone paint.

In the '50s, the trucking industry became the dominant force in commercial transportation of goods. The railroads, which had thrived during World War II's gas rationing, declined in the postwar era. In 1958, freight car loadings fell to their lowest point since before the start of World War II. Dodge's 1958 truck offerings ranged from the sporty Sweptside pickup in the foreground to all types seen behind it.

U.S. factories were running at less than full capacity in 1957 as the economy seemed to be moving into a slight recession. In many cases, the Federal Reserve's tight money policy — cutting government spending to try to balance the budget — was the culprit. Parked outside this Chrysler plant is a 1958 Dodge Royal Lancer four-door hardtop.

Billy Casper Jr., Art Wall and Bob Rosburg were the top golfers of 1959. Casper took the U.S. Open title, Wall was named pro-golfer of the year and Rosburg took national PGA honors. Judging by the sandtrap scene behind this 1959 Dodge D-100 pickup, these are some of the many new amateur American golfers of the era.

Used extensively for military duty during World War II, the Dodge four-wheel-drive "Power-Wagons" were among America's most popular "off-road" vehicles in the '50s. This is the 1959 W-100 half-ton version in two-door suburban (station wagon) format.

This 1959 Dodge Royal Lancer four-door hardtop characterized many styling trends of the mid-to-late '50s, with its hardtop roofline, oodles of chrome trim, two-tone paint, dual rear antennas, whitewalls and jet-plane tailfins.

Plymouth

"Perfectly suited to Summer" says the '50s billboard advertising Jantzen women's swimsuits. A great car to drive to the beach was a 1950 Plymouth DeLuxe convertible.

One Picture...

can never tell Miami's story...a fabulous tropic metropolis...entirely surrounded by sunshine...where more Americans have more fun than anywhere else on earth!

"NO CONTEST..." Miami truly has no equal...is really tropical...hundreds of miles nearer the winter sun...boasting exotic birds, beasts, fish and flowers ...*unique* sightseeing thrills.

RIGHT IN THE CENTER...through access to *all* attractions...a dozen golf courses, miles of ocean beach, acres of parks...superb accommodations at the most favorable rates in the area!

Miami

FOR AMERICA'S BIG VACATIONS!

FREE COLOR BOOKLET...highlights the year-long array of parades, pageants, special events...spectacular, complete... *yours* when you **MAIL THIS COUPON!**

Dept. of Publicity, Literature Section
320 N. E. 5th St., Miami, Florida
54-4

Name_____

Address_____

City_____ State_____

TRAVEL GUIDE—a helpful Oshkosh booklet—FREE! Address *Oshkosh Trunks & Luggage*, Dept. 30-G, Oshkosh, Wisconsin.

MINNETONKA

"SHE ALWAYS GOES HIGH-HAT WHEN SHE CARRIES OSHKOSH"

...and no wonder! For the superb styling and superlative quality of Oshkosh Luggage identify its proud possessors as truly travel-wise—discriminating globe-trotters who know that Oshkosh gives precious possessions superior protection over more years and miles of travel. Zephyr-light in weight...yet brutally strong. Every detail a triumph! From $25.00 to $5,000.00.
IT'S NOT GENUINE OSHKOSH UNLESS IT BEARS THIS LABEL!

none finer 'round the world

Oshkosh LUGGAGE

The accompanying 1954 ad for Miami vacations shows a family carrying beach gear in a Ford station wagon. Switching from high-maintenance wood construction to all-steel bodies made station wagons cheaper to build and handier for everyday use. The 1950 Plymouth Suburban was one of the earliest all-steel wagons.

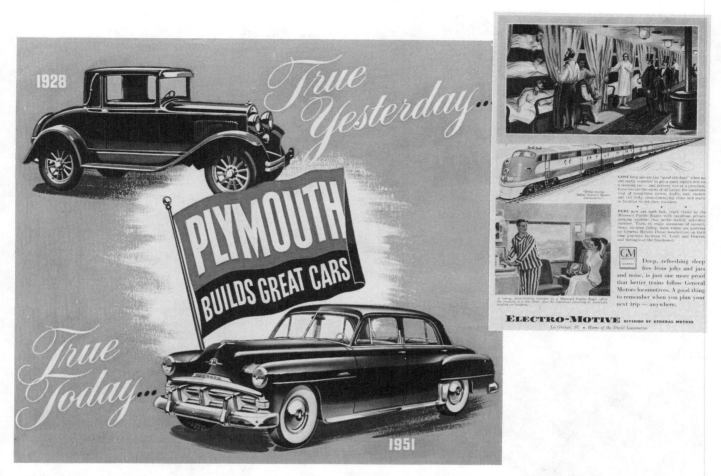

Many '50s ads compared the past and present to show lifestyle improvements and technological developments. On the right, an ad shows railroad sleeping accommodations then and now. On the left, an ad compares the first Plymouth with the latest 1951 model.

The first of a long series of "idea cars" built for Chrysler by Ghia in Italy, the Plymouth XX-500 was custom-built on a 1951 Plymouth chassis.

A total of 83,450,409 pneumatic tires for O.E.M., replacement and export markets were built in 1951. Due to material restrictions caused by the military "Police Action" in Korea, many cars that year lacked whitewall tires when new. This 1951 Plymouth Cambridge two-door sedan has black tires; it was common to see such styles even on billboard ads.

An intense interest in America's "Old West" was evident during the '50s. It popularized dude ranches, TV westerns and ads showing cowboys "rounding up" 1951 Plymouth sedans.

Although streamlined design was a hit in the '50s, the "fastback" or "torpedo" shaped auto body lost favor. People associated cars such as this 1952 Plymouth Concord with the early '40s and considered it outdated.

Beauty in Leather
by WHEARY

Luggage fashioned from rich lustrous leather... incomparably styled... crafted with the skill of artisans... truly a luggage masterpiece. *That is Wheary!*

Previewed above is one of the many models that Wheary will have for you...just as soon as sufficient materials are available to meet Wheary's exacting quality standards.

WHEARY INCORPORATED, RACINE, WIS.

WHEARY
THE NAME TO REMEMBER
IN LUGGAGE

TRAVELERS ARE JUDGED BY THEIR LUGGAGE

Equipment and trim are subject to availability of materials.

"The name to remember in luggage" — according to the accompanying postwar ad — was Wheary. This Racine, Wisconsin firm made high-quality leather luggage, and this salesman could fit lots of it into his 1953 Plymouth Cranbrook business coupe when he removed the rear seat.

The Plymouth Cranbrook Sedan and the Plymouth Savoy,
shown at the Greenbrier, White Sulphur Springs, W. Va.

The architecture of an automobile can kindle a light in its owner's eyes and warm
the pride of possession. As, indeed, the balanced new beauty of the Plymouth does.
And beneath this beauty, unseen, is the integrity of the engineering that created it . . .
a low-priced car, built so well, to look so well, to serve so long and well.

PLYMOUTH

After winning a world war, Americans came home with a sense of national pride that inspired a fascination is U.S. history. This is reflected in advertising art showing a 1953 Plymouth Cranbrook sedan at historic Greenbrier Hotel in White Sulphur Springs, West Virginia.

The Plymouth Explorer was designed by Chrysler stylists and custom-built by Ghia in Italy.

Hats, gloves and handbags were "must" accessories for well-dressed ladies in the '50s. Likewise, the "well-dressed" 1954 Plymouth Belvedere hardtop was accessorized with full-wheel discs, whitewalls and two-tone finish.

MAIL COUPON FOR FREE FOLDER AND

COME TO
LIFE IN
SAN
DIEGO

America's only International Playground

Sail, fish, golf! See Mt. Palomar, La Jolla, Coronado . . . tingle to real foreign excitement in nearby Old Mexico. See our free folder and come to life in San Diego this winter!

SAN DIEGO CONVENTION & TOURIST BUREAU
499 West Broadway, San Diego 1, California, Room 312

NAME _____
ADDRESS _____
CITY _____ ZONE ___ STATE _____
I will come by ☐ Auto . . . ☐ Train . . . ☐ Air . . . ☐ Bus

"Come to California," many ads of the '50s beckoned. Some 13 million people lived there in 1954 when this Plymouth Belvedere Suburban was built, including the 334,387 residents of San Diego. The state's population in 1940 had been only 6,907,387 people.

The Plymouth Belmont was another "idea car" experiment. Its fiberglass body was a roadster type, having no side windows.

This modern ranch home was among 1,320,000 dwellings constructed in 1955, which was a prosperous year with building costs increasing twenty-two percent over 1954. This also meant that more people were buying new cars like this '55 Plymouth Plaza four-door sedan.

Fifty people died on July 25, 1956 when the 29,083-ton Italian luxury liner "Andrea Doria" collided with the Swedish liner "Stockholm" and sunk in the sea forty-five miles south of Natucket Island. The Stockholm and other vessels saved 1,650 lives, but not the Plymouth Plainsman. The show car that Chrysler Corporation had constructed in Italy sunk to the bottom of the Atlantic.

Leading designers agree that **THE FLIGHT-SWEEP** is the car style trend of the future!

PLYMOUTH BELVEDERE 4-DOOR SPORT SEDAN HARDTOP

"This is the direction all car design should ultimately go."
Ted Jones, *boat designer, Slo-Mo-Shun, Miss Thriftway and "X-100"*

"The Flight-Sweep is the freshest approach yet in the evolution of car design."
Edward F. Burton, *Chief Engineer, Douglas DC-8 Jet Transport*

"The Flight-Sweep looks like motion. It's eager, vital with a feeling of the future."
Anne Fogarty, *fashion designer*

All over America there is increasing acceptance of THE FLIGHT-SWEEP, the exclusive design of the 1956 cars of Chrysler Corporation. People agree that the long, low aerodynamic lines from headlight to upswept tail make this the design that others must follow in the years to come. Leading designers in many fields, such as those above, back up this judgment. These experts find THE FLIGHT-SWEEP appealing in its expression of modern living . . . youthful, dynamic. And it has a generous touch of the future!

See and drive the 1956 Plymouth, Dodge, De Soto, Chrysler or Imperial. No other cars offer so much in style, in driving ease, in performance, in *value* . . . and offer it to you *first!*

CHRYSLER CORPORATION ➤ THE *FORWARD* LOOK
PLYMOUTH · DODGE · DE SOTO · CHRYSLER · IMPERIAL

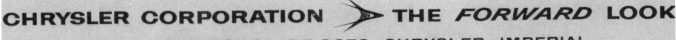

Motorboating produced 1956's biggest sports controversy when Willard Rhode's hydroplane, "Miss Thriftway," won the Gold Cup Race in Detriot, but had to wait three months to get the trophy, due to claims the boat had hit a buoy. Ted Jones — designer of the speedboat — was one of three professionals who hailed "Flight Sweep" styling in this ad for the 1956 Plymouth.

During 1956, a $15,500,000 double wind tunnel was constructed at Langley Field in Virginia to test supersonic aircraft at wind speeds up to 3,800 mph. Do you think it was used to help design the "Aerodynamic Plymouth '56," too?

In the fall of 1957, the Milwaukee Braves won the World Series on Oct. 10 and the Soviet Union launched its second satellite (containing a live dog) on Nov. 3. The 1957 Plymouth shown in this fall scene is a Belvedere four-door sedan.

Famous polo competitions of the late '50s included the Meadow Brook Club of Long Island, New York; Circle F of Dallas, Texas; and Aurora of Buffalo, New York. The sport was catching on. So were sporty cars like the 1957 Plymouth Fury hardtop.

A total of 3.73 million tons of aluminum were produced worldwide in 1957. The United States accounted for 1,647,700 short tons of the lightweight metal. Some was utilized for the "Silver Dart" side spears on this 1958 Plymouth Belvedere four-door hardtop.

"Let's go to the movies to see 'Marjorie Morningstar,' 'Gigi' or 'The Vikings,'" this 1958 Plymouth Fury owner may be suggesting. These were among the year's most popular motion pictures.

The aerospace industry had plenty of jobs for engineers in 1959 as America pushed to close Russia's lead in the "Space Race." This fellow looks like the type who can shoot a rocket straight up but can't straighten his tie. Let's hope he drives his 1959 Plymouth hardtop straight down the road!

Championship cyclists from America included Chicago's Dave Rossi who won the 1959 U.S. Amateur Open Class and Joanne Speckin, of Detroit, who took the Women's Open title. These riders are cycling for exercise and to get a close look at the 1959 Plymouth Sport Fury hardtop.

Ford in the Fifties

Innovations, Triumphs and Milestones

By Peter Winnewisser

Each decade of Ford history is filled to the brim with its own innovations, triumphs, milestones and, occasionally, failures. The 1950s was no exception. Here's a look at a few of the highlights of the Ford Motor Co. story between 1950 and 1959.

1950 — Mercury's showing this year was impressive. The millionth Mercury, a four-door sedan, was produced in August and a new calendar year U.S. production record of 334,081 units was set. In addition, Mercury was selected as the official pace car at the 1950 Indianapolis 500.

1951 — Two firsts marked this year: a fully automatic transmission and the Victoria, a true pillarless hardtop. The transmission was offered optionally as Fordomatic in Fords and Merc-O-Matic in Mercurys. The Ford Victoria was a six-passenger Custom Deluxe two-door hardtop with the V-8 engine.

1952 — Completely restyled Fords, Lincolns and Mercurys were the centerpiece of the Ford Motor Co.'s second postwar generation of passenger cars. Ford also introduced an all-steel station wagon which regained first place from the Plymouth Suburban with 30.9 percent of the output for this body style.

1953 — The 1953 Ford was the 50th anniversary model and the last of the flathead V-8-powered Fords. The final flathead boasted a 7.2:1 compression ratio and produced 110 horsepower at 3800 rpm. This compares with the 65 horsepower at 3400 rpm and a 5.5:1 compression ratio of the first V-8 in 1932.

1954 — A new Ford overhead valve Y-block V-8 rated at 130 horsepower debuted for Ford/Mercury and light/medium truck units. Ford also made truck news by joining its competitors in making factory-installed tandem axle models, the T-700 and T-800.

1955 — Highly prized by collectors today, the legendary two-seat Thunderbird was introduced for 1955 and continued through 1957. Over that three-year span it outsold its rival, Corvette, 53,166 to 10,308. Ford presented the Thunderbird as a "personal" car. But others like Tom McCahill (*True's Automobile Yearbook for 1955*) called it "a full-bore sports car in the finest tradition."

1956 — The Lincoln Continental Mark II (1956-'57) was introduced in Paris in October 1955 as a $10,000 luxury hardtop coupe. It was the most expensive U.S.-made motor car of the time. Noted for its classic simplicity, the Mark II fell victim to a market that was severely limited by its price. It was discontinued in 1957.

1957 — For the first time since 1935 the Ford car outproduced Chevrolet in model year production. Ford introduced the new Skyliner, the first and only retractable hardtop. Like Ford and truck models, the Mercury line was extensively redesigned and featured the distinctive gadget-laden Turnpike Cruiser.

1958 — The 1958 Edsel, a Ford-built medium price car, was introduced in September 1957 and discontinued in 1959 after a run of just 110,847 units, about half of what the company anticipated to produce in the first year alone. It was the industry's most costly mistake to that time.

1959 — The classy 1959 Fords were awarded the Gold Medal for exceptional styling at the Brussels World Fair. For the second time in three years the Ford car outsold Chevrolet. The fifty millionth Ford was assembled.

Edsel

This modern house may have been built in 1958, when some 1,202,000 dwellings were constructed. Unfortunately, construction of 1958 Edsel Ranger two-door sedans wasn't that brisk. Just over 4,600 were made.

One-piece swimsuits, worn with boldly striped beach jackets, were fashionable in 1958. The all-new Edsel Citation convertible was also boldly styled with a distinctive "horse collar" grille.

Fashion designers of 1959 emphasized the width of ladies' figures at the top with such **trompe-z'oeil** devices as oval necklines, as seen on this model's dress. Automotive fashions reflected by the 1959 Edsel Corsair four-door hardtop include heavy chrome trim, wraparound windshield and quad headlamps.

This woman's just-over-the-knee hemline reflected the popularity of "short" skirts in 1959. Knitted sweaters were also "in." A car that never became popular with the "in crowd" was the year's Ranger four-door sedan.

Ford

Golfing vacations (as suggested by the accompanying 1950s advertisement) grew in popularity after World War II. Americans had more leisure time to spend on travel and sports. Shown in a golf course setting is a 1950 Ford Custom Deluxe V-8 convertible.

Feathered hats were a postwar fashion hit with the ladies. The one worn by this smartly dressed woman definitely reflects "high" style. The envelope-bodied 1950 Ford Custom Club Coupe was a style leader, too.

If this 1950 Ford F-3 truck doesn't look like the "fuel" trucks of today, it's because the fuel used to heat many homes back then was coal. During the decade, oil and electric furnaces would replace many of the old coal-fired units.

In the early '50s, Americans felt that the coming decade would be a time of great national prosperity. Many families wanted the best housing available and the latest in clothing fashions. There was an increased emphasis on "deluxe" automobiles, too. Approximately 75-86 percent of 1951 auto production was in this category. Seen here is the 1951 Ford Deluxe Tudor sedan.

Records were broken in the U.S. electric power field during the 1950s, as the nation "turned on" to increased use of time-saving appliances. This 1951 Ford Country Squire station wagon is the more powerful V-8 model with 100 "horses" under its hood.

Casual clothes were "in" for 1952. For men it was pinstripes, flat lapels and solid colored shirts with no ties. Tailored suits, long skirts and the hatless look dominated women's wear. The restyled Fords had a more casual, less boxy appearance as illustrated by this 1952 Customline four-door sedan.

The 1952 dressy look for men was keyed on coordinates with contrasting trousers. Wide ties with rather loud patterns were popular, and hat crowns were getting lower to fit inside the low rooflines on cars like this 1952 Ford Crestline Victoria hardtop.

Outdoor billboard advertising was much more common in the '50s, and this sign highlighted the features of the classic 1953 Ford F-100 pickup truck. Like all 1953 Fords, these trucks had a special horn button commemorating the company's 50th anniversary.

In October 1953, Ford announced that its third quarter sales were the highest since 1929. The sales appeal of the 1953 Sunliner convertible was one reason for the business boom that year. The company also announced and opened a new technical service laboratory in Livonia, Michigan — perhaps the site of this photo.

A specially trimmed Ford Sunliner convertible paced the Indy 500 on May 30, 1953. Bill Vukovich won his first 500 with an average speed of 128.740 mph. The car seen here is an actual pace car and now resides in the Henry Ford Museum and Greenfield Village in Dearborn, Michigan. Replicas of the pace car were built and sold to the public in 1953.

Featured in this display at the Spud City Nationals in Stevens Point, Wisconsin are a number of the most visible symbols of the 1950s' pop culture. They range from a vintage A&W carhop uniform to a snack tray with 40-year-old root beer glasses. The car is a 1953 Ford Crestline Victoria hardtop.

Note the 1953 style road sign. The octagonal shape had been selected as the standard symbol for stopping, but the color red had not been universally adopted yet. The Customline four-door sedan was a real showroom traffic stopper that season, and 374,487 people bought one.

Approximately 4,076,000 American babies were born in 1954 (25.3 per 1,000 citizens). The population boom — prompted by hopes of long-lasting peace and prosperity — made station wagons tremendously popular, and Ford was the leading wagon-maker with thirty-two percent of the market. The car shown is a 1954 Country sedan.

The population living on farms in the United States during 1954 numbered about 22,158,000 folks. This represented a drop of about three million persons since 1950. The workhorse on this modern farm is a 1954 Ford F-100 pickup.

The Eagle Rescue Squad of Little Falls, New Jersey purchased this Ford fire engine in 1954. During that year, major fires in the United States caused over $1 billion of property damage and killed 12,100 people.

Life in the early '50s was often summed up by photos of suburban ranch houses with new cars in the driveways. Population growth in the suburbs ran about 46.5 percent between 1950 and 1954, when this Ford Crestline sedan was built.

American GIs became interested in European sports cars during World War II. The 1955 Ford Thunderbird was an attempt to market a domestic two-seat sports car. Though enthusiasts loved it from the beginning, the T-bird never became a hot seller until it got four seats. Today, however, it stands as a well-known automotive symbol of the fabulous '50s.

"Foxtails" were an accessory that many young motorists added to their '50s cars. According to **Old Cars** *advertising representative Paul Katzke, his insurance company charged higher rates for cars with a foxtail. This restored 1955 Ford Fairlane sedan wears one on its radio antenna to evoke the spirit of the '50s.*

The one-piece look in women's fashion was a 1956 winner. Men's wear moved away from the Ivy League style, but no one told this fellow. However, his madras plaid shirt was "in." So was Ford's sporty T-bird, now featuring a rear-mounted spare tire a la the "continental look."

The wrap-over skylight on the Budd rail diesel car in the attached 1955 ad might have inspired the Ford Crown Victoria's "tiara top" treament. This "Crown Vic," a 1956 model, is ready for rail shipping. It won't have wheel covers installed until it gets to a dealership. During 1956, American railroads dropped $50 million in net income from the previous year.

Ford's technical center was announced in January 1954 and opened in December 1954 in Livonia, Michigan. In addition to modern architecture, it featured an outdoor turntable that helped designers and photographers view cars — such as this 1956 Customline sedan — from various angles.

Small business grew up and prospered in the more service-oriented 1950s. The Small Business Act of 1953 created the Small Business Administration (SBA) to help small firms obtain start-up financing, government aid, and disaster aid. Wendell B. Barnes was the SBA administrator in 1956, when Kent Leitgabel's father purchased this Ford F-100 to use in his plumbing and heating business.

Renting a car on vacation was pushed in this 1957 Avis ad, which notes a cost of $7.50 per day and eight cents per mile for a new Ford rented in Bay City, Michigan. But that's not where the Fairlane 500 sedan was in this photo. This picture was taken in Russia. Wonder what the muscovites thought of this symbol of capitalist wealth?

As you can see by the inset ad, the Avis Rent-A-Car system promoted the driving of new Fords in 1957. Under the company's Fly & Drive Ticket program, the rental cost was $10 for twenty-four hours and fifty miles of use. One car not seen in the typical rental car fleet was the new Fairlane 500 Skyliner "hardtop convertible" with a fully retractable steel roof.

In 1957, the city of Vermillion put this modern Ford C-Series Tilt Cab pumper into service. A $14 million blaze at a rubber reclaiming facility in Butler, New Jersey was that year's largest property-damaging fire. It took place Feb. 27. Nine days earlier, seventy-two people died in a nursing home fire in Warrenton, Missouri.

Hemlines rose to the knees in 1958 and floral prints — mostly roses — were the rage. Home construction revenues rose, for the fourteenth consecutive year, to $34.7 billion, even though the number of new houses built decreased a bit. Another thing that rose that year was the number of headlights. Nearly all U.S. autos, including the 1958 Ford Fairlane 500 Skyliner, had four.

A slight decline in the birth rate from 25.0 per thousand citizens in 1957 to 24.3 in 1958 didn't explain why sales of the 1958 Ford Ranch wagon were down the latter year. The truth is there was still a population boom going on and two-door wagons were a bit inconvenient for families.

"Concerning the design of buildings, it is quite evident that both their profile against the sky and their structural systems are becoming more complex," said the **1959 Funk & Wagnalls Encyclopedia Yearbook.** *The same might be noted of the year's new Thunderbird coupe. It represents a mild face-lift of the all-new four-seat T-bird introduced for 1958.*

A 1958 Ford F-800 heavy-duty truck makes a delivery of bottled soda pop to a Raleigh, North Carolina Gulf service station. Those soda bottles — as well as the wooden crates they are stored in — are collector's items today.

By 1959, motor vehicle registrations in the United States totaled 58.6 million — an increase of forty-two percent from the start of the decade. There were over eighty-two million licensed drivers in the country, but only 12,915 were driving 1959 Ford Skyliner retractable hardtops like this one.

During the late 1950s, service trucks with hydraulically operated "snorkels" were developed for use in utility work and on emergency vehicles. Doug Ogilvy, of Appleton, Wisconsin's Pierce Body Company, was a pioneer in the design of such units. Doug may even have a truck such as this 1959 Ford Snorkel Utility in his large collection of commercial vehicles.

Lincoln

Lincoln used the name "Cosmopolitan" to identify its fanciest 1950 models, such as this coupe. And America was becoming cosmopolitan after World War II. Between 1950 and 1955, the population in metropolitan areas increased from 83.8 million to 95.2 million, a 13.7 percent increase.

During 1950, more than one million new homes were built in America. This marked the third year in a row for such figures. This looks like one of them, with one of the smaller 1950 Lincoln series coupes in the driveway.

This specially built "bubble top" Lincoln phaeton was built in 1950 for President Harry S. Truman. Gen. Dwight David (Ike) Eisenhower was elected President in 1952; he also used this car.

Lincoln's luxurious 1951 Cosmopolitan sedan was promoted by publicity photos — such as this one — that emphasized the good life in postwar America. During 1951, Lincoln put out 390,439 cars, the most since the company's inception in 1922.

During the 1950s, there was outstanding growth in America's telephone system and communications technologies. An emergency telephone system, devised by Bell Laboratories for installation on city streets, flashed a light at a fire station when the receiver was lifted. The car near the telephone poles in this photo is a 1951 Lincoln four-door sedan.

By the end of 1952, Lincoln was building cars like this Capri convertible in three plants. Only Lincolns were made in the Detroit factory. Both Lincolns and Mercurys were produced in a Los Angeles facility. The factory seen here is most likely the brand new plant in Wayne, Michigan, which was scheduled for completion in 1952. Both Lincolns and Mercurys were built there, also.

Ford Motor Company's Lincoln-Mercury Division celebrated the 30th anniversary of the Lincoln nameplate in 1952 with stylish models like the Capri two-door hardtop. Also in style is the lady's fashion ensemble.

The '50s were an age of positive thinking about the future of America. This was reflected in the many "dream cars" — such as the 1953 Lincoln XL-500 — exhibited in new-car shows of the decade.

Dark colored cars like this 1953 Lincoln Capri convertible were losing favor in the mid-1950s. The three most popular colors that year were light blue (13 percent of all U.S. cars); light green (12.4 percent); and light gray (9.7 percent). However, dark green (7.9 percent) and black (7.8 percent) were in the top five.

Custom auto body building virtually disappeared after World War II, although a handful of specials were constructed on luxury car chassis. This is an unusual 1953 Lincoln limousine.

MODERN DRIVING MEANS!

(Performance note: Lincoln again won first four places among all stock cars in Pan-American Road Race.)

response from so light a toe-touch. Never have you known such superb control. For only Lincoln among fine cars gives you ball-joint front wheel suspension for better handling. And you can have Lincoln's power steering, power brakes, the 4-way power seat, and electric power window lifts.

If you like your living modern, if you want to drive the way you live, there is only one thing to do. Accept your Lincoln dealer's invitation to try a Lincoln or the Lincoln Capri. We believe you will never go back to old-fashioned driving!

LINCOLN DIVISION • FORD MOTOR COMPANY

NEW 1954
LINCOLN

DESIGNED FOR MODERN LIVING- POWERED FOR MODERN DRIVING

House parties were in style in the '50s. What better way to show off your modern fashions, modern furniture and modern art? Of course, not everyone drove a 1954 "Road Race" Lincoln right into the center of the party!

114

By 1954, American females outnumbered American males by one million. These women are cruising in their 1954 Lincoln Capri convertible.

When the curtain behind this 1955 Lincoln Capri convertible rises, we might find ourselves viewing one of the year's hot motion pictures, such as "Blackboard Jungle," "The Desperate Hours," "Oklahoma," "Strategic Air Command" or "The Seven Little Foys."

1955 LINCOLN

Features the Spark Plugs of the Future

NEW *TURBO-ACTION*

CHAMPIONS!

The trend continues to history-making new Champion *TURBO-ACTION* Spark Plugs!

The superior performance of these completely new spark plugs in the most advanced engines now has earned their acceptance as standard equipment on the mighty 1955 *LINCOLN*.

Champion *TURBO-ACTIONS* definitely are the spark plugs in *your* future because they solve the number one problem of modern high-compression, high-output engines: low-speed fouling and high-speed pre-ignition. They supply the entire automobile industry with a key to increased horsepower and efficiency for engines of the future.

Because the *TURBO-ACTION* principle involves a larger thread size and an exclusive new seating pattern, these great new Champions can be installed only in those ultra-modern engines designed to use and benefit from them.

Your present car will continue to give you top performance with regular, standard Champion Spark Plugs.

With the *TURBO-ACTION* Spark Plug, Champion once again demonstrates its leadership in spark plug research and manufacture and its ability to anticipate the needs of the automobile industry and the motorist.

CHAMPION SPARK PLUG COMPANY, TOLEDO 1, OHIO

Greater clearance in the firing end permits turbulent gases to keep the insulator free of harmful deposits. Heat range, the temperature zone in which spark plugs operate efficiently, is extended to the widest limits in automotive history.

Exclusive tapered Turbo-Action seating design forms a positive lock with a mating surface in the cylinder head without use of a gasket. Correct installation is automatic and Turbo-Action Spark Plugs remain firmly fixed and accurately positioned in the combustion chamber.

AVAILABLE AT ALL LINCOLN, MERCURY AND OTHER CHAMPION DEALERS

In the 1950s, it seemed as if every feature or part in an automobile had its own catchy name. For example, this 1955 Lincoln Capri is shown here in an ad for Champion "Turbo-Action" spark plugs.

Lincoln tried to emphasize the past, present and future in this publicity photo of its Futura dream car, which was snapped in New York City's Central Park on March 3, 1955.

LINCOLN

The Lincoln Premiere Four-Door Sedan

Have you felt the quiet, sure pride of arriving in a Lincoln?

People who know fine cars admire the clean, gracious beauty of this completely new Lincoln: the longest, lowest, most powerful, most wanted Lincoln of all time . . .

When you arrive in a Lincoln you step out proudly — and with very good reason.

For in the unmistakable Lincoln beauty — a beauty of clean lines and distinctive proportions — there is a clear reflection of your knowledge of fine cars. Obviously, you recognize new trends . . . and you prefer Lincoln's fresh, youthfully modern design.

Beyond Lincoln's beauty, there are so many *other* satisfactions: the conviction, for example, that no other car can approach Lincoln for ease of handling. For there's a personal, effortless feel in the way this big car takes a curve or threads through traffic; so much so that women, especially, say that Lincoln is easier to drive than even a small car — and just as easy to park.

Too, this Lincoln leaves no doubt about its superlative performance. Sweeping down a turnpike or easing into your host's driveway, Lincoln's high-torque, *usable* 285 horsepower teams smoothly and silently with Lincoln's incomparable Turbo-Drive — to put you confidently in command.

Yes, you'll be proud to arrive in a Lincoln, because no other car speaks so well of you.

LINCOLN

Unmistakably . . . the finest in the fine car field

This 1956 Lincoln Premiere advertisement reflects the prosperity of the 1950s. The personal incomes and savings of Americans continued to rise, and savings banks in the United States increased deposits to more than $29.9 billion and total assets to more than $33 billion.

Lincoln organized a brand new Continental Division to sell the classically styled, luxurious 1956 Continental coupe. Although production settled down from the record levels of 1955, the percentage of U.S. families owning automobiles (seventy-four percent) reached an all-time high in 1956.

"Quadra-Lites" were options on Lincoln Premieres in some states during 1957. Other states would not permit their use until 1958. Note how airbrush artists have touched up this photo of the Landau hardtop to add the new safety feature.

Despite the fact that this lady is driving her 1957 Lincoln Premiere convertible facing backwards, deaths from motor vehicle accidents dropped that year. The total of 38,500 compared to 39,628 deaths in 1956.

A slowing of the economy, in 1957, held down sales of luxury cars like the Lincoln Continental coupe. National income was slightly above 1956 levels but reflected an increase of only 0.75 percent in growth of goods produced. Personal income grew more, at five percent, but this was offset by a continued rise in the cost of living which was 2.9 percent, up from 1956. The recession was considered slight because there were too many elements of strength to presage a major downturn.

Wilderness trail in Monument Valley on the Utah-Arizona border.

Firestone lets you follow the lure of lonely trails!

Where it's a ten-mile hike to the nearest help, Firestone ends the danger of tire failure. There's puncture-protection and peace of mind built into every FIRESTONE NYLON SUPREME!

Whether you travel the busy highway or ride the lonesome trail, Firestone makes your peace of mind puncture-proof! You're protected from roadside delays because this tubeless tire's gum liner seals punctures as fast as they occur. An exclusive diaphragm protects from blowout danger by stopping sudden air loss.

Wherever you drive, add peace of mind to your travel plans. Order your new car with Firestone Nylon Supremes®, or trade in your present tires at your nearby Firestone Dealer or Store.

Firestone

BETTER RUBBER FROM START TO FINISH

Exclusive diaphragm retains 67% of air in tire even if blowout occurs. Gum liner seals punctures permanently.

Copyright 1957, The Firestone Tire & Rubber Company

A 1957 lincoln traveled the wilderness trail in Monument Valley (on the Utah-Arizona border) to test puncture-proof Firestone Nylon Supreme tires. This was a banner year for replacement tire sales with an all-time record of 56.5 million units shipped. OEM tire shipments were 32.5 million, up 1.6 million from 1956.

121

Classic elegance in motorcars: The Lincoln Premiere Landau. Gown by Traina-Norell.

THE NEW LINCOLN . . . inspired by the Continental

the one fine car that lets you rediscover the rewards of exclusive fine car ownership

For the first time in many, many years, there is a new, *exclusively different* motorcar in the fine car field.

The new Lincoln — styled and crafted in the classic Continental tradition — is the one fine car that sets you apart from the commonplace.

It is the one fine car that combines clean, classic beauty with large size . . . the one fine car that is impressive without being ostentatious.

It is a superb, exciting car to drive . . . a car that will let you rediscover the pleasures of lux-

urious motoring. The engine simply whispers — for all its 375 horsepower. The body and frame are a single, solid unit — so that you may have lasting quietness over any terrain. And all about you, the decor of the interior is one of tasteful, classic elegance.

If, like so many others, you are seeking a fresh new kind of distinction in fine motorcars, this new kind of Lincoln for 1958 is the car you have been waiting for.

LINCOLN DIVISION, FORD MOTOR COMPANY

Unmistakably . . . the finest in the fine car field

THE NEW CONTINENTAL MARK III . . .
inspiration for The New Lincoln

The belle of the ball in 1958 was likely to come in a custom-designed gown by Traina-Norell. And when she left, it was likely to be in a Lincoln Premiere Landau, the car that "sets you apart from the commonplace."

At Dinner Key, near Miami, Mr. Scott interrupts a brief vacation to pose for a picture with his Lincoln Landau. Here in Florida, as in every other marine vacation area, his company's famous Evinrude and Johnson outboard motors enjoy unmatched popularity among power-boat owners.

"I have a keen interest in this business of pleasurable travel. And Lincoln excels at it,"

Mr. Scott is pictured in front of the Outboard Marine Corporation office building. This handsome new structure reflects his corporation's dynamic growth in recent years—from sales of 27 million dollars in 1947 to almost 160 million dollars in 1958.

says *William C. Scott, president of Outboard Marine Corporation — world's largest producers of outboard marine motors.*

William Scott is not only a specialist in pleasurable ways to travel—he also has a discerning eye for design excellence, for precision workmanship and meticulous attention to detail. And, as a highly successful business leader, he is not unaccustomed to the finest automobiles.

Knowing this, we are especially pleased that he chose Lincoln. The graceful distinction of this car's uncluttered lines first attracted him. And once behind the wheel of his Lincoln, he discovered a magnificent handling quality, a silken-smooth obedience to his slightest touch.

Moreover, inherent in Lincoln's superb design are extremely wide door frames for easy entrance and exit. You sit in seats that are wider, too, and the height of an armchair. You are surrounded by specially loomed fabrics, hand-cut leathers, resplendent coachwork.

If you appreciate an uncommon dedication to your comfort, combined with an equal dedication to expert craftsmanship—then this is the year to change to *Lincoln.*

Lincoln

Classic beauty...unexcelled craftsmanship

LINCOLN DIVISION · FORD MOTOR COMPANY

At Dinner Key, near Miami, Florida, William Scott — president of Outboard Marine Corporation (America's largest producer of outboard marine motors) — shows off his '58 Lincoln Landau. OMC grew from sales of $27 million in 1947 to $160 million in 1958, reflecting the national emphasis on leisure and vacation activities during the '50s.

"Easiest role I ever played on the road: touring in my new Lincoln." Helen Hayes

"I'm only five feet, two inches tall," admits actress Helen Hayes. "Most big cars overpower me. But not my new Lincoln. It seems so gentle and easy I could almost drive it through a display of crystal and not break a single glass."

The 1959 Lincoln offers all the power and comfort you expect in a big car. Yet it handles like a fine sports car. Just a touch, and the Lincoln responds to your slightest whim. The new small steering wheel is easy to turn and easy to see over. Nothing gets between you and perfect visibility.

"I had so much fun decorating my new Lincoln. I chose the exact colors, fabrics and leathers I wanted."

You enjoy complete freedom of choice when ordering your new Lincoln. You select from ninety different color combinations, each more beautiful than the last. You choose from rich fabrics or imported leathers to complement the exterior. The result—a motorcar built especially for you ... the 1959 Lincoln.

The Lincoln Premiere Coupe

"The space in this car! Sit any way you like, it's simply impossible to feel cramped."

Among fine cars, only Lincoln provides beautiful classic styling without sacrificing interior space and comfort. Heads never touch the ceiling, feet never crowd the floor. Yet for all its spaciousness, any woman maneuvers the new Lincoln as easily as a shopping cart.

"When we drive up to the theater, people recognize the Lincoln first —then me! I'm sure it's no jealous. It's such an elegant car."

Whenever you see the 1959 Lincoln, you expect to find people of even finer taste. The new Lincoln's clean, uncluttered design speaks a classic language, understood by all who live with grace and elegance.

Lincoln for 1959

Classic beauty...unexcelled craftsmanship

LINCOLN DIVISION • FORD MOTOR COMPANY

A Broadway hit of 1958 was "A Touch of the Poet," a production of the last posthumously published Eugene O'Neill drama that lent distinction to the theater season. It was still playing in 1959, when actress Helen Hayes drove to "work" in her Lincoln Premiere coupe.

Mrs. Igor Cassini says: "I believe the Lincoln has more chic than the other fine cars."

"It's a matter of personal taste. But to me, its simple elegance makes it more beautiful."

Naturally, we agree with Mrs. Cassini, wife of society spokesman Cholly Knickerbocker. After all, we designed the 1959 Lincoln for people whose tastes lead them to the trim, the elegant and the uncluttered.

If you are accustomed to the finest, we believe you'll enjoy seeing and driving the 1959 Lincoln soon. And when you do, you will notice immediately another striking difference between the Lincoln and other fine cars. Simply this: *Lincoln, for all its beauty, has not sacrificed an inch of comfort and spaciousness.*

For one thing, it's easier to get in and out of a Lincoln. The wider door frames are designed for graceful entrances. And once inside, you'll find almost four more inches of shoulder room. In the back seat, some models are almost a third of a person wider. The seats are the height of a comfortable easychair, thanks to the Lincoln Uniframe Construction. You never feel awkward or cramped.

The things we have talked about are important to people like Mrs. Cassini. We believe they should be important to you and every other fine-car buyer. Won't you make a comparison between Lincoln and other fine cars? Sit in them. Drive them. We think you'll agree: *this is the year for you to consider making the change to Lincoln.*

Mrs. Igor Cassini — wife of society spokesman Cholly Knickerbocker — had no trouble parking her 1959 Lincoln in New York City. Perhaps she was heading to the theater to see Sidney Poitier in "A Raisin in the Sun" or Paul Newman in "Sweet Bird of Youth."

125

"Design is the vital thing—
and Lincoln proves it beautifully,"

says planebuilder Donald Douglas,
chairman of the board, Douglas Aircraft Company.

Donald Douglas seated in his office with models of two of his most famous planes, the DC-3 which made aviation history—and the DC-8 jetliner, another Douglas masterpiece of design soon to be introduced.

World pioneer and already legendary leader in aircraft production. Dynamic designer and engineer. Rugged individualist. Sportsman. This is the man who directs Douglas Aircraft. The kind of man for whom we planned and built the magnificent 1959 Lincoln.

A man who responds to Lincoln's classic, dramatically simple lines. And who can fully appreciate the luxurious spaciousness provided in this distinctive design. A spaciousness that lets you step in and out with ease. That gives you more head room and elbow room, more leg room and foot room than any car in America.

And Lincoln furnishes its spacious interiors with unparalleled elegance. You sit in seats the height of a fine armchair, *and equally as comfortable.* You are surrounded with specially loomed fabrics, handcrafted leathers soft as a glove, superb coachwork.

Donald Douglas, a man accustomed to the finest, is quick to recognize value and distinction and refinement. We invite you to do as he did—compare Lincoln with any of the other fine cars. We feel sure that you, too, will find this is the year to change to Lincoln.

During 1959, an estimated 55.6 million passengers traveled on U.S. airliners. Domestic carriers added 313 jets to their fleets for a total of 2,063 commercial aircraft. Many of the new planes were DC-8s produced by Donald Douglas, who is seen here with his 1959 Lincoln.

General Romulo is pictured in front of his office in Washington, D.C., with his Lincoln Premiere Landau.

"Its simplicity of style – its distinctiveness – these are what I like about Lincoln",

says General Carlos P. Romulo,

soldier, statesman and diplomat

For decades, important figures in Washington have chosen Lincoln as their motorcar. And the 1959 Lincoln is no exception.

Designed for persons of importance everywhere, it is a magnificently built automobile. Distinctive, tasteful, original. Built to assure superb handling ease and roadability. Built with a meticulous craftsmanship that is reflected in even its smallest appointments. Built to give its owner unparalleled luxury and elegance.

For example, Lincoln is the roomiest six-passenger motorcar in the world. Its wider doors make it remarkably easy to step in and out. Lincoln's seats are also wider than those of other fine cars, and the height of a comfortable armchair.

If your preference is for an automobile with dramatically simple lines and complete attention to your comfort, you may find this is the year for you to make the change *to Lincoln.*

General Romulo was Fourth President of the United Nations General Assembly, aide-de-camp to General Douglas MacArthur in World War II, and Pulitzer Prize-winning journalist. Recently, the Freedoms Foundation of Valley Forge honored him with the Freedom Leadership award for 1958.

Lincoln

Classic beauty...unexcelled craftsmanship

LINCOLN DIVISION · FORD MOTOR COMPANY

The 14th session of the United Nations General Assembly convened on Sept. 15, 1959 and adjourned Dec. 13. Gen. Carlos P. Romulo, the fourth president of the General Assembly, is seen near a 1959 Lincoln Premiere Landau outside his Washington, D.C. office.

Mercury

The war was over and Americans were anxious to indulge themselves after years of rationing and material shortages. Among the products they bought were the "complete home entertainment" console made by Admiral and a 1950 Mercury convertible to drive to the country club.

Actor Clark Gable was an American heartthrob in 1950 — as well as a car buff. On May 30, he showed up at the Indy 500 to ride in the 500 Parade in a 1950 Mercury "official car."

This attractive advertisement by the Budd Company of Philadelphia depicted the trains, cars and trucks the firm built after the war. "Generic" cars in the painting reflect some of the postwar styling motifs found in this 1950 Mercury four-door sedan.

Station wagons gained popularity as the "baby boom" exploded in the '50s. This type of dual purpose car was extremely popular with the 25,150,000 Americans who lived on farms when this Mercury woodie wagon was built in 1951.

The young man shown on this '50s style billboard obviously deserves that tall glass of Sunkist lemonade after mowing the lawn behind the 1952 Mercury Custom sedan.

Due to Korean War material restrictions, the availability of white sidewall tires was extremely limited. That's why the 1952 Mercury Custom Sport Coupe shown here lacks such tires.

Over 1.5 million marriages took place in America during 1953. One of the longest lasting was Mercury's mating of a powerful V-8 engine with the stylish Monterey two-door hardtop model.

The custom car hobby was a big fad in the '50s. One of the most popular cars to "personalize" was the hot-performing Mercury. This 1953 convertible has the teardrop spotlights and "flipper" hubcaps that customizers loved.

Surviving today in the well-known collection of '50s dream cars founded by Chicago's Joe Bortz is the futuristic (in 1954) Mercury XM-800.

This 1950s billboard design promoted shopping in the Yellow Pages, but these women look as if they'd rather go shopping in this 1954 Mercury Monterey sedan!

Vista-Dome trains, like the "California Zephyr" (see inset ad) inspired the glass-topped 1954 Mercury Sun Valley hardtop.

Open the curtains behind this 1955 Mercury Montclair convertible and you might find the postwar General Electric "Musaphonic" FM-AM radio phonograph seen in the accompanying advertisement.

Slim coats with lavish outsize collars — often fur-trimmed — kept American women warm in 1955. The same was true of the toasty heater-defroster available in this 1955 Mercury Montclair sedan.

Everyone read **Modern Screen** to get the latest gossip about Marilyn Monore. In 1956 — when this Mercury Monterey sedan hit the showrooms — the blonde sex symbol married playwright Arthur Miller. She also starred in "Bus Stop."

It's surprising that the owner of this 1956 Mercury Custom convertible couldn't find a nice set of reasonably priced whitewall tires to dress it up. Tire sales dropped six percent that year, and retailers were offering consumers good prices on whitewalls.

No book about the '50s would be complete without photos of the decade's fabulous "dream cars." This is the 1956 Mercury XM-Turnpike Cruiser.

The always popular 500-mile race at the Indianapolis Motor Speedway grew and grew in the '50s. Perhaps part of the reason was a record birth rate in 1957 — 25 babies for every 1,000 citizens!

Coats made of short-haired fleece or monotone tweed (such as seen here) were fashionable during 1957. However, for cars like the Mercury Turnpike Cruiser, a two-tone coat of paint was all the rage.

For 1957, the world's most famous auto race — the Indy 500 — was also called the Indianapolis Motor Sweepstakes. Sam Hanks took the checkered flag, averaging 135.601 mph. A Mercury Turnpike Cruiser convertible carried the 500 Festival Queen around the speedway during pre-race ceremonies.

This rendering of the glittery 1957 Mercury Turnpike Cruiser could be set in the equally glittery Hollywood hills. Some of movieland's big hits that season were "Teahouse of the August Moon," "Pal Joey," and Elvis Presley's first film — a Civil War drama called "Love Me Tender."

Boating and yachting buffs cheered when the U.S. vessel "Columbia" took the 1958 America's Cup, winning four races from the "Sceptre" of England. This sailor gives some navigational tips to the owner of a 1958 Mercury Turnpike Cruiser.

The 1958 Mercury Colony Park station wagon wasn't a great seller. Perhaps that's because the birth rate that year was 24.3 per 1,000 people — a decline from 25 per 1,000 in 1957.

In 1959, the world production of mercury increased from 245,000 flasks in 1958 to 248,000 flasks. Of course, we're talking about "quicksilver" — not automobiles like the Mercury Montclair hardtop shown here.

Conoco stressed longer lasting lubricants in this 1959 billboard. Although Mercury did not recommend 50,000 miles between oil changes, this woman motorist was likely to drive her 1959 Mercury Park Lane farther than ever without major service.

General Motors in the Fifties

A Car for Every Pocketbook

By Pat Chappell

The fabulous '50s was an exciting decade for General Motors. The corporation continued to field five separate divisions: Chevrolet, Pontiac, Buick, Oldsmobile and Cadillac. The divisions ran the gamut from everyman's car to luxury on wheels. In between were three choices which carried out Chief Executive Officer Alfred P. Sloan's dictate: "A car for every pocketbook."

This field of five divisions made GM strong enough to handle just about any situation the economy dished up. These five completely self-contained "houses of manufacture" formed formidable competition for Ford Motor Co., Chrysler Corp. and the independent manufacturers. Because of GM's size and its diversity, it was to establish a position of powerful leadership in the '50s. By 1955, GM controlled 50.8 percent of the market.

It was a magic time for the automobile industry, particularly at GM where the vice president of automotive styling, Harley J. Earl, combined forces with Harlow P. Curtice, executive vice president of GM in 1948, who rose to president of GM by 1953. Add to that one of the best engineering groups in the country with men like Harry Barr and Ed Cole, and success was certain.

Harley Earl provided leadership in the styling field, which influenced the rest of the industry, and he'd been doing that through the '30s and '40s. He defined his mission: "My primary purpose for 28 years has been to lengthen and lower the American automobile, at times in reality and always at least in appearance."

Earl had an actual showcase for his styling exercises in the form of a traveling Motorama show which ran from 1953 through 1961. The GM Motorama toured major U.S. cities and attracted several million people. It was at these shows that the production Corvette, Chevrolet Nomad and Cadillac Eldorado Brougham were first introduced as dream cars. The shows were spectacular Hollywood-type extravaganzas, described by one automotive writer as "artful manifestations of lingering dreams."

Rivaling the importance of the Motorama shows was the completion of the GM Technical Center in Warren, Mich. by 1956. It was a high water mark of industrial design which housed GM's styling and engineering staff.

In its role of leadership in the '50s, GM established an impressive list of achievements and records. Consider the trend set by the tiny graceful fin on the '48 Cadillac, and the '49 Buick Riviera, which was the first U.S. two-door hardtop to enter production. The 1950 Chevrolet was first in the low price field with a two-door hardtop *and* automatic transmission. In 1952 Cadillac and Buick celebrated their 50th anniversaries. GM's 50 millionth production vehicle was a '55 Chevrolet Sport Coupe. In 1956 Pontiac celebrated its 30th anniversary. By 1957, Oldsmobile celebrated its 60th anniversary. In 1958 GM was 50 years old. By 1958, the two millionth Cadillac rolled off the assembly line.

What an impressive numerical display of production milestones, anniversaries and longevity! GM was king, and the American automobile ruled the road. These *were* the fabulous fifties!

Buick

The clothing worn by the Duke and Duchess of Windsor and the "Palm Beach" bumper badge are both typical of the early '50s focus on more leisure time. The 1950 Buick Super Estate wagon has Florida vacation car written all over it!

Buick entered the '50s as America's fourth-best-selling car. The brand was popular with fast-rising professionals who weren't quite in the Cadillac income bracket. Anxious to flash their new success, these early "yuppies" loved Buick's flashy portholes and bucktooth grille. The Super had three portholes. This is the 1950 four-door sedan.

This publicity photo for the 1951 Buick Super convertible brings back memories of the popular postwar TV series "The Bob Cummings Show," which traced the amorous exploits of a professional photographer.

Newspaper gossip columnists of the '50s often wrote about goings-on in romantic places, such as the French Riviera. Buick adopted the term "Riviera" to identify its pillarless hardtops. Here we see the 1951 Roadmaster Riviera coupe. Also notice that though the sleek Buick reflects the new '50s focus on produced styling, the lawn mower in the background does not have a "designer" look.

This XP300 show car was produced for Buick by General Motors in 1951.

The 1951 Buick LeSabre dream car was designed by Harley J. Earl, then General Motors vice president in charge of styling. Earl is shown here behind the wheel, driving a visiting diplomat around the GM Technical Center.

Have you ever noticed how all the businessmen in vintage factory photos resemble Ronald Reagan or Robert Young? This staged publicity shot of the 1952 Buick Super Riviera coupe is a good example. Don't ask who the third fellow looks like.

Shortly after World War II, the West Coast hobby of personalizing automobiles grew into the custom car industry, and car designers from Detroit began attending custom car shows to get new styling ideas. One of them was Buick's Ned Nickles, who utilized customizing techniques to create the limited-edition 1953 Buick Skylark convertible shown here. This rare '50s machine was advertised as an anniversary edition to mark the 50th birthday of General Motors. Skylarks were also very expensive ($5,000), and many did not sell for several years.

In addition to portholes along the hood (three on Specials and Supers; four on Roadmasters), another typical '50 Buick styling distinction was the mounting of the radio antenna at the center of the windshield header. This 1953 Roadmaster four-door sedan had a completely new V-8 below the hood. V-8s — so typical of the '50s — were also used in Supers, while the economical Specials stuck to the traditional (for Buicks) overhead valve straight eight.

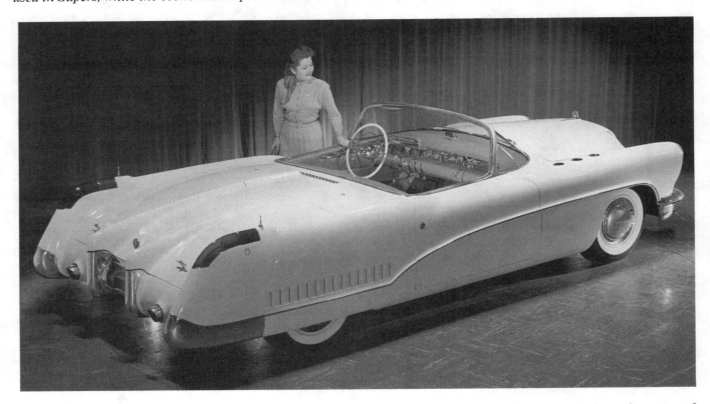

The 1953 Buick Wildcat I dream car was a fiberglass-bodied two-passenger roadster. It was the first of a series of Wildcat dream cars and rode on a 114-inch wheelbase. An unusual feature was the "rotor-static" front wheel discs that remained stationary while the front wheels revolved.

During the '40s, automakers began building futuristic "dream cars" to present their advanced styling concepts to the public. The early '50s was an era in which some of the dream cars were actually sold as limited production models. The 1954 Buick Skylark convertible is one example.

Short shorts and long skirts were all the rage in 1954. So was the all-steel station wagon, which suited the postwar push for easier maintenance much better than the old "woodies." This Buick Century Estate wagon also fit the leisure lifestyle Americans envisioned following the close of the Korean conflict.

Imported sports cars started gaining popularity in the early '50s, and Buick stylists were quick to adopt some of their appearance features. The genuine wire spoke wheels and enlarged rare wheel openings seen on this 1954 Riviera coupe gave it an Italian sports car flavor.

This Buick Roadmaster Landau dream car for 1954 had a blue leather-trimmed chauffeur's compartment with electric division window. The rear of the roof lowered hydraulically like a convertible top, revealing a passenger compartment trimmed in beige leather with mouton carpeting. The rear armrest held a cocktail set and shaker.

The 1954 Buick Wildcat II show car resembles an early Corvette. It's a two-seater on a 100-inch wheelbase with a 322 cubic inch 220 hp V-8. Styling features include an oval grille, flying buttress fenders and porthole hood.

*Broderick Crawford almost always drove a Buick squad car in his '50s hit TV series "Highway Patrol." The CHP actually used 1955 Buicks that were built especially for the law enforcement agency. These police cars were the **only** Century two-door sedans available that year, and just 268 were made.*

Like the modern house behind it, this 1955 Buick Super Riviera coupe had an image of casual luxury. While its pillarless roofline was anything but stiff and formal, its cloth and Cordaveen interior spoke of richness and good taste.

Games such as tennis, golf and shuffleboard attracted Americans who found themselves with more leisure time in the '50s. In automobiles, the "ragtop" — or convertible — emphasized having fun. One of the best-looking ragtops was Buick's 1955 Century model.

Sporty "carriages" of the mid-'50s were a far cry from the horse-drawn types of earlier eras. The first four-door pillarless hardtops from Buick bowed in 1956 in the Special and Century series only. They were offered in the Super (above) and Roadmaster series beginning in 1956.

As illustrated by the accompanying ad from a 1950s magazine, voyages to foreign lands via ocean liners were big in the '50s. You may even remember the hit TV show "Oh, Suzanna." The 1956 Buick Special station wagon was the perfect luggage-toting car.

The 1956 Buick Centurion dream car had a bucket seat that automatically moved backwards whenever the door opened. The body was molded in fiberglass, the grille and hood forming one complete unit, hinged at the front.

Another styling motif that was taken from the appearance of aircraft was the split-window look adopted for some 1957 Buick and Oldsmobile models, such as this Century two-door Riviera coupe.

Aircraft design also had a major influence on automotive styling in the '50s. It was seen in the wraparound windshield, turbine-style wheel covers, simulated rear brake cooling vents and tailfins of the 1957 Buick Roadmaster convertible.

The early '50s brought America the two-door hardtop — which many people at the time called a "hardtop convertible" because it had the sporty lines of a ragtop. The mid-'50s added the four-door hardtop as a sporty family car. In 1957, Buick carried things one step further with the "Caballero," a hardtop-styled station wagon.

America celebrated its 350th anniversary in 1957. The accompanying ad from Sinclair Oil Company highlights the celebration of the founding of Jamestown, Virginia in 1607. An historic setting also seems to be the backdrop of this publicity photo showing Buick's latest Super Riviera four-door hardtop's low-slung silhouette.

Continental tire kits first evolved as a customizer's tribute to the classic 1941 Lincoln Continental. In the early '50s, aftermarket "continental kits" were offered for most U.S. cars. By 1958, Buick had its own very ornate version available for installation by dealers.

Architecture took off in new directions during the '50s. And some might have believed it took an architect to design this "houseboat-sized" 1958 Buick Limited four-door hardtop. Resurrecting a nameplate from the '40s, the ultra-plush Limiteds came in three styles — Riviera coupe, Riviera sedan and convertible — that measured eight inches larger than Roadmasters and all cost over $5,000.

In 1958, chrome seemed to be the pagan idol of the decade of extravagance. And possibly no cars outdid the year's more expensive Buick in their use of chrome trim. This is the Roadmaster Riviera sedan — not even the top of the line!

Customizers of the '50s used chrome-plated dresser drawer knobs to create unique grilles in cars they restyled. For 1958, Buick brought its own version of the "drawer-pull grille" to new-car showrooms. It's seen here on a 1958 Century convertible.

More tasteful use of chrome and more emphasis on sheet metal sculpturing characterized the 1959 Buick Invicta convertible. The use of aluminum was growing in 1959, and General Motors was a force in the move to aluminum auto parts such as grilles and trim. At the time, the emphasis was on the light metal's weather-resistant properties rather than entirely on weight savings.

That's right — back in the '50s they used dogs to drive the pace cars at the Indianapolis 500. And if you believe that, we have a bone to pick with you!

A Buick Electra 225 convertible paced the Indianapolis 500 on May 30, 1959. During the '50s, Indy pace cars were supplied by local dealers — rather than Detroit — and they were rarely copycatted and made available in replica form to the public.

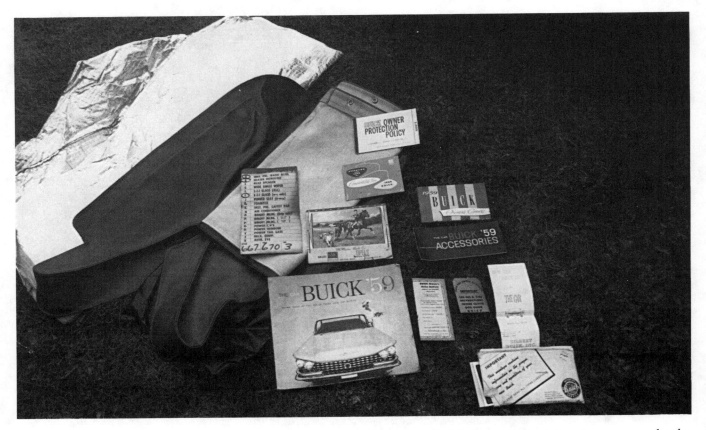

Among the many automotive artifacts that '50s car buffs collect are oil stickers, owner's manuals, accessory books, sales brochures, warranty booklets, showroom and service department tags and even a 1959 calendar sent out by Buick dealers.

This period photo shows the crew that captured the 1959 Indianapolis 500 on film — most likely made by Kodak — for posterity. The men kneeling appear to have some serious equipment at their disposal — but we don't know about the cameras slung around the necks of the other two shutterbugs.

Dashboards of 1950s autos were reflective of the decade's interest in high style and gimmickry. The 1959 Buick instrument panel is a glittery example of the aircraft-inspired school of design. Note the "trick" vertical automatic transmission quadrant above the steering column.

Interiors of late 1950s cars — such as the 1959 Buick Invicta convertible — were wide, spacious, glittery and colorful. Accessories — such as the under-dash tissue dispenser — are collectible today. All that legroom was "standard equipment."

Da, da, da, da — Batman! The TV series hadn't bowed yet, but the 1959 Buick was every inch a mass-produced Batmobile!

Cadillac

Cadillac was America's largest supplier of hearse and ambulance chassis during the '50s. The nearest competitors earned only half as much business from "professional car" builders. This Miller Meteor Cadillac looks prepared for any medical emergency. It's on one of 1,975 commercial chassis that Cadillac sold in 1955.

Cadillac's overhead valve V-8 made it one of the hottest-engined cars of 1950. Here we see four Cadillacs that competed in the 1950 Mobile Gas Economy Run. The three sedans are 1950 models and all racked up over 22 mpg. The 1949 limousine at the rear could do only seventeen miles per gallon.

Back in the '50s, two-door hardtops were often called "hardtop convertibles." Cadillac's Series 62 Coupe deVille is one of the cars that pioneered this '50s body style. This is a 1950 edition.

Custom coach-crafted auto bodies were rare to see after World War II, but a few shops continued to operate on "movie star" business. One of them was the California firm called Coachcraft, which turned out this one-of-a-kind Cadillac station wagon.

Broad lapels and polka dot ties were fashionable for men in 1951. Women preferred Scottish plaid skirts and jackets. While lifestyle changes tooks place after World War II, a Cadillac sedan was always fashionable.

The U.S. government enforced automobile price ceilings and material restrictions during the Korean conflict in the early '50s. Even Cadillacs — such as this 1952 Series 62 coupe — were commonly seen wearing black sidewall tires.

Here's another black-tired 1952 Cadillac. Even with the "conflict" in Asia (no one wanted to call it a war), America's attention was still fixed on the "good life." Caddy convertibles and Florida vacations were everyone's dream.

We recall the early '50s as a friendly time, when Americans felt optimistic about the nation's future. This friendly fellow is driving a 1953 Edlorado convertible. It took a lot of optimism to spend $7,750 for such a car back them.

Black marble was a favorite with 1950s architects and interior designers. But white sidewall tires returned to normal availability in 1953, as fighting wound down in Korea. This 1953 Cadillac Coupe deVille even has genuine wire wheels.

Playing off the new national pride that American fighting men inspired by their performance in World War II and Korea, Cadillac turned to a patriotic backdrop to picture its 1954 Series 62 four-door sedan.

Political slogans such as "I Like Ike" reflected the positive spirit of the mid-'50s. America's soldier-president enjoyed at least one Cadillac Eldorado sports convertible. This 1954 "Eldo" drop-top had a sticker price of nearly $6,000.

Cadillac built more limousines than any other 1950s automaker. This 1955 Series 75 edition sold 841 copies. Another 1,075 seven-passenger sedans were produced the same season. They were essentially identical, but limousines had a division between the front and rear compartments.

Richly brocaded fabrics set off the interior of 1956 Cadillacs. Typical '50s touches included a deep-dished steering wheel, "Panoramic" windshield and bright metal instrument panel grille. Over 86 combinations of fabrics, vinyls and leathers were offered to buyers of different Cadillac models.

Among the dream cars brought to life by GM in the 1950s was the 1957 Eldorado Brougham. This "suicide" door-styled four-door hardtop pioneered pencil stripe whitewall tires and wore a unique brushed stainless steel roof.

New-car shows drew millions of Americans to brightly lit convention halls where the lastest "Detroit Iron" was showcased. This display — very typical of the '50s — highlights the Cadillac line with the 1957 Eldorado Brougham on a revolving turntable.

Patios were the "thing" to add to your home in the 1950s. And having a 1957 Series 62 Cadillac convertible parked nearby didn't hurt the American success story image one bit.

Building designers of the '50s often tried to let their imaginations carry them away. Car stylists tried to do the same. Sometimes they overdid it. The year 1958 was known for styling excesses and untasteful use of chrome trim. Cadillac fared better than many other margues. This 1958 Sedan DeVille is rather subdued in appearance, except for the new grille.

Auto factories still looked quite factory-like in 1958, when this Cadillac Series 62 ragtop was photographed outside one. Cadillacs also looked quite Caddy-like from 1950-1958 with a "family resemblance" throughout the nine-year span. This would change in 1959!

Those 1959 Cadillacs must have looked pretty wild in this rather conservative setting — probably the lobby of the GM Building in Detroit. The typical automobile showroom of the era looked far more modern. Note that the fellow on the right even has two-toned shoes.

It wasn't too much chrome that made critics feel that 1959 Cadillacs went overboard on good taste. It was too much tailfin! However, enthusiasts always loved the special flamboyance of the design — and still do.

Chevrolet

In 1950, the Chevrolet Fleetline two-door sedan was a holdover from the "fastback '40s." It was also available with four doors. The streamlined style was partly inspired by trains like the Santa Fe Super Chief shown in the accompanying 1950 advertisement.

To update its image for the "Fab '50s," Chevrolet introduced the Bel Air hardtop and Powerglide automatic transmission in 1950. The suburban setting for this 1950 Bel Air is a reminder that these regions would grow 46.5 percent in population between 1950 and 1955.

The fabulous '50s marked the height of popularity of sedan delivery trucks, which were well-suited to the postwar boom in small private businesses. This is Chevrolet's 1951 version of the small businessman's favorite delivery vehicle.

Ranch homes were springing up across the nation in 1951. So were Chevrolet four-door sedans, the best-selling automobiles in America. This Deluxe model sports chrome trim and fender skirts.

After the war, several smaller new firms entered the specialty auto body business, turning out limousines, hearses and ambulances based on less expensive cars. This 1951 Chevrolet hearse comes from Guy Burnett of Memphis, Tennessee, a city where several such firms were located.

Believe it or not, the low rooflines on cars like this 1952 Chevrolet Bel Air actually affected men's clothing styles of the '50s. By 1955, fashion writers would note that "the crowns on men's hats were lowered for easier entry into sporty two-toned pastel hardtop autos."

Amazingly, the Chevrolet Fleetline fastback lasted through 1952, with the four-door version disappearing first and the two-door — such as this one — going last. The "torpedo" body look that gained popularity at the start of World War II was over 10 years old and considered passé.

Chevrolet shattered tradition by bringing the Corvette from a "Motorama" show car to production line model in record time. Though its "Blue Flame Six" and Powerglide automatic transmission were not up-to-date sports car features, the fiberglass body shell was visually and technically futuristic.

By the mid-'50s, sixty-four percent of all rural roads in America were surfaced. This brought country folks and city folks closer together and made the cargo-carrying station wagon more popular. This 1953 Chevrolet 210 Townsman was one of three different trim level wagons offered that model year.

During 1954, U.S. air carriers flew 16,768.7 million estimated domestic revenue passenger-miles and 3,744.2 million international revenue passenger-miles. Delivering cargo to this TWA airliner is a 1953 Chevrolet Suburban Carry-All.

The top on this 1954 Chevrolet Bel Air convertible wasn't the only thing down in that year. The economy suffered a downturn during 1953-1954, too. At the time, economists called it a "mild depression." Today, we'd say it was a recession.

Between 1950 and 1955, America's farm population fell by three million people, which raises the question: Is this 1954 Chevrolet stake truck making deliveries or moving a farm family's furniture to the city?

California was America's fastest growing state in 1955. Its population increased by 2.5 million people between 1950 and 1955 — it totaled 13 million in July of the latter year. This 1955 Chevrolet Bel Air Sport Coupe wears California license plates.

The 1955 Chevrolet Nomad personified several automotive trends of the '50s: It was a dream car brought to production; it had sporty styling; luxury was a keynote of the design; and it was a station wagon (what minivans represent to American families today).

Commercial air travel continued to grow in 1956, when 200 new airliners were delivered to American carriers. That was an increase from 113 planes in 1955. The lines of this 1956 Chevrolet 210 Sport Coupe — not to mention its hood ornament — were inspired by aircraft design.

The number of civilian aircraft sold during 1956 reached 7,500, compared to only 4,823 a year earlier. An all-new Corvette sold well, too. Deliveries hit 3,467 versus just 700 in 1955.

In 1957, some Americans drove their Chevy Bel Air convertibles to the beach to get away from it all. Others spent their leisure time taking in hit motion pictures including "Peyton Place" with Lana Turner, "The Spirit of St. Louis" with Jimmy Stewart, and "12 Angry Men" with Henry Fonda.

After introducing the high-style Nomad station wagon, Chevy came out with the Cameo Carrier sport/luxury truck, such as this 1957 example. Females outnumbered males by about 1.5 million that year, and these slab-sided and dressed-up pickups played more to feminine eye appeal.

Feathered hats were all the rage in 1957 fashions. Short jackets, belted snugly at the waist, accompanied long, tight skirts with "vented" hems. A new word in America's vocabulary was "motel" — a contraction of motor hotel. And new from Chevrolet this year were tall tailfins, such as on this 210 model two-door sedan.

New construction in the United States during 1958 increased about one percent to $48.8 billion. The structure behind this 1958 Chevrolet Delray two-door sedan looks almost brand new.

America's female population was estimated at 87,858,000 in 1958, representing 50.5 percent of the total population. This helped make many women more independent. "I'll wash my '58 Chevy myself," says this gal.

Golfers Billy Casper, Arnold Palmer, Ken Venturi and Dow Finsterwald won 13 tournaments and a combined $186,000 in 1957. Maybe they played the course in the background behind this 1958 Chevy Impala convertible.

In the courtyard at GM Styling at the Technical Center, here is Harley J. Earl, then vice president in charge of styling, with GM's 50th anniversary 1958 passenger cars. Earl supervised the design of more than 35 million cars during his career with GM that began in 1927. The Chevrolet is in the foreground. Behind it, left to right, are Pontiac, Oldsmobile, Buick and Cadillac.

Golden milestone cars: Here are GM's 1958 cars as they appeared on the memorable two-hour "General Motors 50th Anniversary" television show presented Nov. 17, 1957 to officially begin GM's Golden Anniversary celebration. Here they are teamed with then equally high-fashion women's clothing. Clockwise from the Chevrolet in the left foreground are Oldsmobile, Buick, Cadillac and Pontiac.

Well-suited to the suburban lifestyle, the all-new 1959 Chevrolet El Camino combined the looks of a contemporary passenger car with the practicality of a truck. The suburban areas growing fastest that year were in Florida (up seventy-two percent since 1950), Arizona (up sixty-five percent) and Nevada (up seventy-five percent in 10 years).

Translucent lighting, prefabricated curtain walls and pre-cast concrete overhangs were keynotes of 1959 architectural trends. The "architecture" of Chevrolets adapted some of the same motifs with overhanging roofs on four-door hardtop models. And how about the cat's-eye taillamps and gull-wing rear end on this Bel Air Sports Sedan?

Softly collared necklines away from the neck were "in" for the ladies in 1959. Hairstyles for women leaned towards short in front, with a high-piled crown. Men went for the collegiate look. Of course, the 1959 Corvette also stressed modern style, plus hotter performance than ever before.

Oldsmobile

TLC 28136.0.0

...mericans got their first chance to fly in an airplane — courtesy of Uncle Sam. During ...nore flying — both privately and commercially. This pilot traveled to the airport in a

This advertisement from the early '50s promotes family vacations in Florida. The 1950 Olds 88 Futuramic convertible was the perfect car for the drive south.

187

Fashionably dressed for winter, this woman pats the hood of her trusty 1951 Oldsmobile, knowing it will start on the first crank because she paid heed to Standard Oil's "Winter Red Crown" gasoline billboard advertising.

Golfing gained great popularity after World War II. An early '50s ad from the Canadian Pacific railroad highlighted the sport. A sporty car to take to the links was the 1951 Oldsmobile Super 88 convertible.

This 1946 advertisement from the All-Year Club of Southern California promotes vacations there. During the '50s,
many Americans relocated to the Golden State. This 1952 Oldsmobile factory photo shows several attractions of the
California lifestyle.

A billboard promoting the "Rootin' tootin' power" of Delco batteries may explain why the owner of this 1952 Olds Super 88 wasn't afraid to drive it far from nearest service station. All GM cars used Delco batteries as standard equipment.

During the '50s, stock car racing grew into a legitimate sport as former "moonshine" delivery experts took their hot V-8-powered cars to the speedways. Milwaukee Oldsmobile dealer John Quaden supplied this 1953 Super 88 convertible to serve as pace car during a race at the city's State Fair Park.

A postwar ad from Gar Wood Industries shows one of the firm's classic wood speedboats. Another classic of the postwar era was the 1953 Oldsmobile Fiesta convertible — a limited-edition, top-of-the-line sports model.

Manmade furs were a fashion hit of the mid-'50s. Garments such as this woman's hat and scarf were easier to care for than real furs. Also easier to care for was the 1954 Olds Starfire convertible.

This 1954 Oldsmobile owner looks ready to leave for the ballroom in her 1954 Olds 88 two-door sedan. Perhaps she was planning to save a dance for Mr. McNutley (Ray Millard), who danced across American TV screens each week in the '50s.

The United States won golf's Ryder Cup and Walker Cup events in 1955, and Cary Middlecoff of Memphis, Tennessee took the Augusta Masters title. Seen at a golf course with plenty of palm trees for shade is a 1955 Olds Super 88 Holiday hardtop.

AIR CONDITIONED S.S. Delta Queen

LUXURY CRUISES THRU
"the heart of America!"

FALL CRUISES TO NEW ORLEANS, LA. *20 Days—Ohio and Mississippi Rivers Lv. Cinti., O., Oct. 2 and 23, 1954.* A fall trip to New Orleans aboard the gracious, air conditioned S. S. DELTA QUEEN is a delightful way to spend a "late" vacation!
You'll enjoy hotel-like pleasures, excellent meals aboard this luxury river steamer . . . thrill to nature's autumnal handiwork . . . explore romantic river towns—and then gay, charming, memorable New Orleans! *Fare $275 up plus tax.*

1955 MARDI GRAS CRUISE. *Reserve space now. Three weeks. $325 up plus tax.* The S.S. DELTA QUEEN is your hotel during four exciting festival days in New Orleans. *Lv. Cincinnati Feb. 12, 1955. Ret. Mar. 5.*

The inset ad from the mid-'50s promoted Mississippi River cruises. It looks as if these vacationers took their 1955 Olds Super 88 sedan with them to Louisiana, a popular tourist attraction during the '50s.

A popular Michigan tourist attraction in the 1950s was the Scenic Dune Rides along the shore of Lake Michigan. The Sleeping Bear Dunesmobile fleet consisted of 1956 Olds Super 88 convertibles.

This woman's two-tone outfit matches the two-tone finish of her 1956 Olds 88 Holiday coupe. Her closed shoes reflected a move, that year, away from open toe pumps and backless mules.

Outdoor activities boomed in the '50s. This period billboard features a hunting theme. Also gaining great popularity was camping. This 1957 Olds 88 Fiesta wagon is outfitted for the great outdoors.

The big yachting news of 1957 was Richard S. Nye's twin victories in the Newport-to-Santander (Spain) Trans Atlantic Race and England's Fastnet Cup. His yawl "Carina" captured both contests for a record second time. A lavish "land yacht" offered by Oldsmobile that year was the Ninety-Eight convertible.

About 1,170,000 non-farm housing units were started during 1958 — a gain of twelve percent from the previous year. This new home has a new 1958 Olds Super 88 Fiesta wagon in the driveway.

In concert musicland, American pianist Van Cliburn won the international Tchaikovsky competition in Moscow during 1958. A bit closer to home, this couple visited their local band shell in a 1958 Olds 98 convertible.

The driver who parked this 1959 Olds 88 convertible by a golf course may have gone to watch Bill Casper win the year's U.S. Open. In Colorado Springs, nineteen-year-old Jack Nicklaus (the second-youngest winner) took the U.S. Amateur Championship.

For dressy occasions, the ball gown made a revival in 1959 — often with a revealing neckline. With its large wrap-around windshield and increased glass area, the 1959 Olds 98 sedan was also of more revealing style.

Pontiac

Immediately after the war, conversion of factories to peacetime production made both cars and tractors hard to get. By 1950, however, this farm family could purchase a new Pontiac Streamliner sedan-coupe or have a new Massey-Harris tractor demonstrated right on the farm.

These 1950 motorists may be smiling because they've just heard that Americans were living longer. The death rate that year — 9.6 per 1,000 people — was the lowest ever. It had dropped ten percent since 1940, the government said. This 1950 Catalina also had a long life expectancy. Pontiacs were known as "the cars that last 100,000 miles."

During the winter of 1951, Gordie Howe of the Detroit Red Wings National Hockey League team broke Herb Cain's previous single-season point record total of eighty-two. The 1951 Pontiac Eight Streamliner station wagon was a great car for family travel during the winter holidays.

Miss Popularity of 1951 was singer and actress Doris Day, whose "Lullaby of Broadway" album was a hot seller that year. The owner of a "25th anniversary" 1951 Pontiac Catalina was also bound to be popular with the younger set.

Consumer spending rose in 1952 as Americans' after-tax income leaped over ten percent. But sales were not keeping pace with the rise in income, causing what the media called an "inflation gap." These citizens were doing their part with a new home and a new 1952 Pontiac Chieftain Deluxe four-door sedan.

In 1952, New Jersey planned a new program to curb habitual traffic violators through a point system that could lead to suspension of drivers' licenses. That may have prompted these winter vacationers to drive their 1952 Pontiac station wagon slower and more safely.

When Italian fashion designer Fontana announced the opening of a New York salon to show clothes especially designed for U.S. women, it became clear that America was looking to the continent for new style trends. For cars such as the 1953 Pontiac Chieftain DeLuxe convertible, a continental tire kit was fashionable, too.

"Something a lady appreciates" was the message used in the Texas Company's 1950s billboards to attract people to Texaco gas stations. This lady also seems appreciative of the 1953 Pontiac Chieftain Deluxe two-door sedan owned by her visitors.

The U.S. Department of Labor and Commerce put building construction in the country, during 1954, at $36,960,000,000. Outside this fancy new home we see a 1954 Pontiac Star Chief Custom sedan.

Great for COLOR!

Contessa 35

A pocket-size miniature with built-in ASA exposure meter and auto-focusing range-finder. Takes 20 or 36 pictures on a load of 35 mm. film. Fast-acting controls, designed to prevent error. T-coated Zeiss Opton Tessar f/2.8 lens is highly corrected for color and black-and-white. Synchronized shutter has speeds to 1/500 sec. See the Contessa 35.

ZEISS IKON

At leading dealers. Write for literature.

Carl Zeiss, Inc., 485 Fifth Ave., New York 17

This man appears to be using an older box-type camera to photograph his 1954 Pontiac Star Chief Custom Catalina hardtop. But more modern 35mm cameras — such as the Contessa 35 — were gaining popularity at this time.

During 1955, the state of Florida adopted a new highway code revising the administration of state roads and established a high school driver education program. Many Americans — including the owners of this 1955 Pontiac 860 two-door station wagon — enjoyed vacationing under the Florida palms.

During 1955, the fifty-three-foot-long Rhodes centerboard yawl "Carina" triumphed in five major yachting events. Richard S. Nye, of Greenwich, Connecticut, owned the vessel. In automobiles, a "winning" design was the 1955 Pontiac Star Chief convertible.

Color coodination was important in clothing and automotive fashions in the mid-'50s. Note how this model's gloves, shoes and sun hat coordinate with her sheath dress. Note, too, that her 1956 Star Chief Catalina coupe has a very coordinated look in design, color and trim.

This fashion model's blouse is boldly done in contrasting color patterns. So is the 1956 Pontiac Star Chief convertible she's posing beside.

This woman looks as if she might be returning from a visit to a hospitalized relative or friend. There were 6,818 hospitals in the United States the year that her 1957 Pontiac Super Chief Safari station wagon was built. During that year, 19,999,262 persons were admitted to hospitals.

The cost of new construction of industrial buildings was $3.2 billion in 1957, a gain of 2.8 percent from the previous year. Parked outside a modern looking auto factory — a new Pontiac Super Chief four-door hardtop.

During 1957, studies were made to determine ways and means to increase the safety of motor vehicles, and shock-absorbing bumpers were one item studied. This Pontiac Star Chief convertible has extra rear-impact protection in the form of a factory-installed continental tire kit.

Driver Jim Bryan won the Indianapolis 500-mile race on May 30, 1958, with an average speed of 133.791 mph. He drove the famous "Belond Special." The official pace car that year was a 1958 Pontiac Bonneville convertible with an optional "Tri-Power" V-8 engine.

An interest in small dogs, as reflected by the accompanying Ford billboard design, was apparent in the late '50s. Popular breeds ranged from Pekingese to miniature poodles. The owner of this 1958 Pontiac Bonneville Sports Coupe was backing the trend with her large — but still lovable — poodle.

Lawn patios were "in" with the suburbanite set in 1959. But not everyone parked his 1959 Pontiac Catalina Sport Coupe out on the patio.

These 1959 Pontiac Bonneville station wagon owners probably took a portable radio along on their picnic. Among the songs they were likely to hear were "Battle of New Orleans" by Johnnie Horton, "Dream Lover" by Bobby Darin, "The Chipmunk Song" by David SeVille and "Charlie Brown" by the Coasters.

The Independents in the Fifties

A Decade of Great Turmoil

By Bill Siuru

The 1950s was a period of great turmoil for the independent automakers. In 1950, Kaiser, Frazer, Hudson, Nash, Packard, Studebaker, Willys and even Crosley were going strong. By 1960, the only one of these nameplates left was Studebaker, and it too would be gone by the mid-1960s.

This was also the decade of mergers and acquistions as the independents tried in vain to survive the competition from the Big Three. Willys-Overland was purchased by Kaiser-Frazer, Nash and Hudson merged into American Motors, and Studebaker and Packard were briefly married in a merger.

Another tack for survival was the independents' attempt to carve out what today would be called a "niche" market. In 1950, Nash brought America's first truly successful compact car, the Rambler. Kaiser followed with the 1951 Henry J, Willys and its Aero models by 1952, and the Hudson Jet appeared in 1953. These were all far less successful and only the Rambler lasted beyond 1955.

The mid-1950s saw the first of Detroit's horse-power races. All the independents, except Willys and Crosley which had already departed the scene, put performance-oriented cars in their dealer's show-rooms. Kaiser attempted to compete by bolting on a surpercharger to its "Super Sonic Six" for its 1954-1955 Manhattans. Packard kept pace first with its own 352/374-cid V-8s and then by supercharging the Studebaker 289-cid V-8 offered in the 1957-1958 "Packabakers." Hudson, with it famous Twin-H sixes, by now greatly outclassed, was relegated to using Nash's V-8s in 1955 through 1957. Studebaker ably competed with its 289-cid V-8s (supercharged for 1957 and 1958) and Packard's 352-cid V-8. Incidentally, in 1951 Studebaker was the first American automaker to offer a modern OHV in a low price car. However, American Motors won the 1950s performance race, at least for the independents, when it shoehorned its 327-cid V-8, 255-horsepower engine into the lightweight Rambler four-door hardtop to create a limited edition, 1957 Rambler Rebel.

The 1950s was also a decade when styling innovations sold cars. Fins were in throughout the 1950s and the independents almost all grafted them on to keep aging designs fresh a year or two longer. Even the Henry J sprouted tailfins. GM brought out wrap-around windshields in 1954. Hudson, Nash, Packard and Studebaker had them by 1955. The same went for quad-headlamps, three-tone paint jobs, sculptured body work and "Reynolds-Wrap" side moldings. Many times, these ad hoc additions created monstrosities from a previously attractive, if not handsome, basic design.

The independents did create a few pace-setting designs in their own right usually on very limited design budgets. The Packard Caribbeans and Kaiser Darrins immediately come to mind. And then there were the Raymond Loewy-designed Studebaker Starlight and Starliner coupes that debuted in 1953, probably the most handsome and innovative styling of the decade from any American automaker.

Checker

Checker Motors of Kalamazoo, Michigan, was never regarded as a leader in advanced automotive styling. This is the company's 1950 long wheelbase sedan — a visual throwback to pre-World War II times. Of course, the company's entire 1950 output was devoted to taxicab production, so functionality and reliability were what Checker buyers wanted.

By the end of 1956, there were 62,275,000 motor vehicles in use in America, and traffic jams were becoming a national problem. "Ride relaxed-free from driving strain" said a period ad promoting the use of Greyhound buses for intercity travel. In urban areas, one answer to strain-free transportation was the boxy-but-comfortable 1956 Checker cab.

Crosley

"Bigger is better" was a prevalent notion during the fabulous '50s, but some products reflected the opposite point of view. For home movie buffs, Kodak offered the "Medallion 8" pocket-sized camera weighing only 23 ounces. Small car fans might have gone for the 1950 Crosley station wagon, which tipped the scales at 1,403 pounds.

Frazer

As you can tell by the dress worn by this model, there were major changes in women's fashions between 1950 and the close of the decade. The 1951 Frazer Manhattan actually looks more modern than the clothing styles shown in this publicity photo.

During the '50s many projects — such as the construction of four gigantic hydroelectric generators (the largest ever built) at the McNory Dam on the Columbia River — were initiated to insure America's future needs for electricity. Seen behind this rare 1951 Frazer convertible sedan is a power line of the type that carries electricity from such generators to American homes.

Henry J

A version of the Henry J was sold in Sears, Roebuck department stores as the Allstate. It had a fashionable plaid plastic interior. Speaking of fashion, do you think these models are wearing styles from the 1952 Sears catalog?

With America's economy booming in the '50s, "bigger and better" was the type of slogan that sold cars. The diminutive Henry J, such as this 1953 model, was a high-quality compact car that never caught on.

Hudson

This restored 1950 Hudson Commodore Eight four-door sedan has many popular postwar accessories: wheel trim rings, white sidewall tires and a spot lamp.

While the house and model's dress in this publicity photo seem a throwback to prewar times, the 1951 Hudson Pacemaker sedan characterizes the company's all-new postwar styling.

DON'T FRY
THIS SUMMER

HAVE REAL AIR CONDITIONING in your bedroom or office tomorrow

TELL the weatherman to bring on his heat waves. You won't mind a bit when you have one of these new Fedders Room Air Conditioners in your bedroom or office window. Fedders is real electrically refrigerated air conditioning at a new low price you can easily afford. Sits on your window sill, plugs in like a radio. No ducts, no water connections, no building alterations needed. Cools and dehumidifies the air, filters out dirt, dust and pollen. Don't wait for hot, sticky weather. See your Fedders dealer today. Mail coupon below for complete details.

fedders
A GREAT NAME IN COMFORT

New low-priced model now available in Hawaiian Tan . . . the season's smartest color.

"Don't fry this summer" was the message in the accompanying 1950s ad for a Fedders home air conditioner. These pretty ladies avoided frying by putting down the top on their 1951 Hudson Hornet convertible and cruising to the lakeshore.

Sleeveless tops and long, swirling skirts were fashion hits of 1952. Always fashionable is a speedy convertible, such as this 1952 Hudson Wasp.

Two-tone paint schemes were very much a part of automotive marketing during the 1950s. This 1952 Hudson Hornet sedan has upper and lower body two-toning.

A brief wave of compact car enthusiasm evolved in the early '50s as manufacturers recognized increases in the number of woman drivers and two-car families. The 1953 Hudson Super Jet was among the group of small cars that failed to catch on at the time.

Hudson dressed up the compact Jet and sold it as the Jetliner in 1954. This car buyer is also dressed up for her trip to the showroom. Fashion trends that year included straighter skirts, shorter coats and "Audrey Hepburn" hair styles.

The latest in automobile interior fashions is demonstrated by a fashionably outfitted 1954 Hudson Jet owner.

During the early '50s, the Hudson Hornet was widely recognized as a hot performer. This 1954 convertible, supplied by Milwaukee County Hudson dealers, was the official pace car for a stock car race held at that Wisconsin city's State Fair Park.

Real furs — except mink — slumped in popularity in the mid-'50s as manmade furs (knitted of dynal and orlon) took over. They were lighter in weight and easy to clean. Also slumping badly were sales of Hudson automobiles, such as this 1954 Hornet Special sedan. During that season, Hudson would merge with Nash to form American Motors Corporation.

Little half-hats that clamped to the top or back of a lady's head were commonly seen in the mid-'50s. The model in this publicity photo for a 1954 Hudson Hornet wears such a chapeau.

World War II gave America a global perspective and sent more citizens traveling throughout the world. Ads — like this one for Italian tourism — filled the pages of magazines. This new "continental" mind-set inspired automakers to turn to Italian design studios for limited-production models such as the '54 Hudson Italia. In 1955, over a half-million Americans would go to Europe.

California led all states in total population increase with a gain of nearly 2.5 million people between 1950 and 1955. Two of the state's 13 million residents of the latter year are seen here with their typical "SoCal" home and rather typical 1955 Hudson sedan.

The 1950s was an era of ornamentation and textures. Exposure to modern surroundings brought about a revolution from the past quarter century of constrained living and dressing. Both clothing styles and car styles grew flashy and racy. The 1955 Hudson Wasp is a good example of the new look of these days.

The lady on the left wears a high waistline dress that was considered chic in 1956. Her friend's outfit reflects the trend in women's sportswear — sweaters and skirts dyed to match. Also in style with its bright tri-tone paint scheme is the 1955 Hudson Hollywood shown here.

These fashionably dressed ladies might be heading for the movies in the 1956 Hudson Wasp sedan. Films likely to be playing at the Bijou included "War and Peace," "Giant," "The Ten Commandments," and "Around the World in 80 Days." Each of these epic hits was more than three hours long.

Outer space was on everyone's mind in 1957, the year that Russia launched two Sputniks — the first man-made satellites — into orbit around the earth. The 1957 Hudson Hornet V-8 had its own version of out-of-this-world styling with airscoops, tailfins and abundant chrome trim.

Kaiser

Two generic cars — resembling an Oldsmobile and a Hudson — showed up in a 1950s advertisement for Hartford Insurance. This 1951 Kaiser Deluxe Club coupe had safety features designed to prevent accident damage — such as the largest glass area in the auto industry and a padded instrument panel.

Stylist Howard "Dutch" Darrin gave the 1952 Kaiser Manhattan a sculptured look similar to the streamliner trains promoted in a Union Pacific Railroad ad from the same period.

During World War II, "Rosie the Riveter" helped symbolize the American woman's new-found freedom from occupational stereotypes. This 1954 Kaiser-Darrin exhibit, at an auto show, carried this concept one step further.

America's tennis heroines of the mid-'50s included Louise Brough of Beverly Hills and Beverly Baker Fleitz of Coral Gables, Florida. Either of these cities would have been the perfect place to drive a 1954 Kaiser-Darrin sports car. This pioneer fiberglass body car had unique forward sliding doors.

Why is an accident investigation vehicle parked next to the 1954 Kaiser-Darrin loaded with beauty queens? Was someone worried that they would distract passing drivers? In the '50s, beauty pageants and prom nights were catching on as America's postwar culture grew more and more youth-oriented.

Located just north of the United States Air Force Academy in Colorado Springs, Colorado, this '50s style auto dealership was still repairing Kaisers when this photo was taken in the 1980s. The car is a 1954 Kaiser Manhattan.

Nash/Rambler/AMC

The Great Lakes played a vital role in the U.S. postwar economy, serving as both a tourist attraction and a shipping route. A view of Lake Erie was used to promote vacations in Ohio in the early '50s, while Nash Motor Company — located in Kenosha, Wisconsin — relied on a giant lake freighter to ship these 1950 Ramblers to market.

During the '50s, the Great Northern Railway advertised vacation trips to Glacier National Park in the Montana Rockies. There tourists could ride a sight-seeing bus that had the same roof treatment as this 1950 Nash Rambler convertible.

"Are you going to the lake or the shore for vacation this year?" was a question heard often in the fabulous '50s. Minnesota's tourist department used a cartoon to promote travel to the "Land of 10,000 Lakes." Parked by the side of a Wisconsin lake is a 1951 Nash Ambassador Custom sedan.

The early '50s brought increased interest in the history of America, which was reflected in "traditional" clothing styles. Note the similarity between the ball dresses shown in an early '50s ad for the Louisiana Spring Fiesta and the publicity photo of a 1951 Nash Rambler two-door hardtop.

For Travel Memories
You'll Cherish Always

See *Italy* first

ITALIAN STATE TOURIST OFFICE—E.N.I.T.
21 East 51st Street, New York 22, N. Y.

USA 1952

"See Italy First" said an ad trying to lure Americans to Venice in the early '50s. World War II had introduced many G.I.s to the beauty of the Mediterranean nation, and their war stories sparked interest in traveling there. This 1952 Nash was styled by Italian designer Pininfarina and was photographed in his country.

When dining out in the '50s, men wore jackets, ties and hats. This duo may have had to remove their chapeaus inside their small 1952 Nash Rambler Greenbriar station wagon.

Houses with two-car garages became a reflection of changing lifestyles in the '50s. Smaller cars, such as this 1953 Nash Rambler station wagon, were aimed at the two-car family market.

Greyer Advertising used billboards to promote the carrying capacity of 1953 Nash automobiles. The Nash Rambler Country Club hardtop had a continental tire, which also increased trunk room.

This advertisement compared the design and "Airflyte" construction of the 1953 Nash to that of modern buses, planes and trains of the era.

About $12,912,000,000 worth of private, non-farm residential building was completed in 1954. The owners of this 1954 Rambler Country Club hardtop may be among the many Americans who went house-hunting that year.

This fashionably attired model demonstrates the clothing styles of 1954, the year that Nash merged with Hudson to form American Motors Corporation. The Rambler Custom sedan would retain its Nash nameplate until 1957. This is a 1954 model.

This model donned short shorts to stay cool while washing her 1955 Nash in Crown Point, Indiana.

About 1,320,000 dwelling units were constructed during 1955, the year that this Nash sedan was sold. Like the modern home behind it, the car is long, low and two-toned.

NOW YOU CAN HAVE A
Beautiful Lawn
QUICKLY, EASILY

Rotary MOW-MASTER Mower

MOW-MASTER mows lawns beautifully
Cuts tall grass and weeds easily
Pulverizes Autumn leaves instantly

Mow-Master keeps the lawn fresh and clean spring, summer and fall. It cuts fast, saving valuable time. It pulverizes clippings, abolishes raking. **The Only Mower with the amazing Grind-a-Leaf attachment for Autumn Lawn Cleaning.**

• 2 H.P. Engine
• Direct Drive
• Finger tip control
• Easy to maneuver
• Adjustable cutting height

PROPULSION ENGINE CORP. (Dept. NG-5)
7th ST. & SUNSHINE RD., KANSAS CITY 15, KANSAS

Gentlemen:
Please send me your illustrated folder, describing the MOW-MASTER Line of Power Mowers and Grind-a-Leaf attachments.

NAME

ST. ADDRESS

CITY   STATE

Write Today for literature on the Mow-Master Line.

"Now you can have a beautiful lawn," advertised the Propulsion Engine Corporation of Kansas City, Kansas in the mid-'50s. Perhaps one of the firm's Mow-Master rotary mowers was used to keep the lawn behind this 1956 Nash Ambassador Country Club hardtop so neatly trimmed.

A lack of rain caused a major drought over a huge area of the United States during 1956. Perhaps that explains the small amount of snow on the ground in this photo of an Ambassador Special V-8 released by American Motors' Nash Division on April 2, 1956.

In 1957 women's golfing competition, JoAnne Gunderson took the U.S. amateur title and Betsy Rawls won the National Women's Open when Jacqueline Ping was disqualified. The women in this photo took their 1957 Nash Ambassador Super sedan to the country club for a round of golf.

Perhaps these women forgot to fill their 1957 Rambler Custom Country Club station wagon with Esso Extra and ran out of gas. As the period billboard suggests, Esso advertised "long distance power" as a feature of its premium grade fuel.

American Motors Corporation (AMC) was formed as a result of the merger of Nash-Kelvinator and Hudson. Just before the start of the 1958 model year, the Nash and Hudson names were dropped in order to concentrate on the revised series of cars called the Rambler. The 1958 Rambler American, a revival of the 1955 Rambler, was offered only in a two-door sedan for 1958.

AMC was the only major U.S. automaker to increase sales in the recession year of 1958. The consumer trend was to smaller cars, and the Rambler was the only U.S. compact. The car above is a 1958 Rambler Rebel Custom four-door hardtop sedan.

The 1959 Rambler American continued as a compact model with smooth, rounded styling that dated to 1953. This is a '59 American two-door sedan.

Did women really shop for groceries in heels and gloves in the 1950s? In 1959, the two-door station wagon was revived for the Rambler American line.

Rambler registrations doubled for 1959, even though the 1959 Rambler Ambassador retained the same basic styling seen in 1958. This is a 1959 Ambassador four-door hardtop.

This 1959 Rambler Ambassador Custom station wagon features the four-door hardtop styling pioneered by Rambler three years previously.

Ranch-style houses gained in popularity throughout the '50s because they were easy to heat and cost less to build than conventional two-story dwellings. This 1959 Rambler Rebel Custom station wagon has woodgrained applique within its side trim spears and sports a roof rack.

Rambler utilized fins, too, in the 1950s. These bright metal-trimmed fins on the 1959 Rebel Custom four-door hardtop are evocative of those on contemporary Mercedes-Benz.

Packard

The Packard Predictor is another of the famous '50s dream cars built for the auto show circuit.

Did you know Goodyear Tire & Rubber Co. made luggage in the early postwar years? This prototype 1950 Packard station sedan could have held a lot of Neolite suitcases.

Judging from her binoculars, this woman may be an ornithologist. Perhaps she's looking for a cormorant on the front of the 1950 Packard, but this model has a stylized hood ornament that's less bird-like.

Travelers in the early '50s carried more luggage than most of us take along these days because auto or rail travel took longer. As you can see, the 1952 Packard Patrician sedan offered immense trunk space for everything from suitcases to golf clubs.

Picture Yourself

in
MISSISSIPPI
the hospitality state

You don't need to be a camera fan to
enjoy the refreshing variety of scenery
at any time in Mississippi. Picture yourself at historic Vicksburg overlooking Ol'
Man River . . . at Natchez with its lovely
ante-bellum homes . . . fishing in a cy-
press-studded Delta lake, or sunning on
a Gulf Coast beach. You can picture
this and more, but you can't visualize the
warm welcome you'll receive in this tradi-
tionally hospitable state. Write for complete information.

SEND FOR NEW 4-COLOR PICTURE FOLDER

Miss Hospitality
Travel Department, NG-12-53
State of Mississippi
Jackson, Miss.

Please send
me the new all color folder
and illustrated map covering
your attractions.

Name
Address
City   Zone   State

*The skies are gray and the lake is misty, but this daydreaming woman might be thinking about a summer vacation
in Mississippi (see inset ad). Her 1951 Packard 200 hardtop would be great for making the trip down south.*

Characterizing the image of a successful 1950s businessman is this middle-aged fellow. His fedora, double-breasted jacket and shoes are right in style — as is his 1951 Packard 200 sedan.

The Traymore Hotel in Atlantic City, New Jersey was an historic landmark "Renowned the World Around" according to '50s advertisements. But most postwar travelers found motels better suited to their needs and budgets. In addition, they could park their 1952 Packard 200 coupe right outside the doors.

"Meet Springtime in St. Petersburg" read an ad for Florida vacations in 1953. Judging by the foliage behind her, this 1953 Packard Clipper sedan owner took the ads seriously.

Successful businessmen (note his wife's fur coat) found the luxury of the 1954 Packard Patrician appealing. However, a mild depession from mid-1953 to mid-1954 hurt both U.S. business and Packard sales.

Television helped popularize golf in the '50s and led to an explosion of driving ranges nationwide. This 1954 Packard Clipper Super Panama hardtop was owned by someone who wanted to practice a proper swing.

Styling motifs seen on the limited production 1954 Packard Caribbean convertible were taken from the Santa Fe Railroad's diesel Streamliner. Fred G. Gurley, president of the Santa Fe Railroad system, was a pioneer in modern motive power equipment. The railroad's Super Chief, Chief, El Capitan, Grand Canyon, Texas Chief and California Limited trains helped promote travel to the West in the '50s. They offered sleeping accommodations and Fred Harvey cuisine.

Industrial construction for 1954 totaled about $1,968 million with many new factories built. However, the Mitchell-Bentley facility where Packard's Panther dream cars were made was far from modern and new. (Courtesy Joe Bortz)

Golfer Jack Fleck of Davenport, Iowa won the 1955 National Open golf tournament. This golfer looks like a winner, too. His wife is picking him up in a 1955 Packard Clipper Constellation hardtop.

This 1950s ad (inset) promoted travel to Southern California. These residents of America's fastest growing region took advantage of one of its best features — sunny weather — by lowering the top on their 1955 Packard Caribbean convertible.

Off to see "The Solid Gold Cadillac" in their two-toned Packard Patrician are three fashionably attired women. The 1956 hit motion picture starred Judy Holliday and Paul Douglas.

William Mitchell, president of Mitchell-Bentley Corporation in Ionia, Michigan, stands beside the Packard Daytona show car he built for the automakers to use as a "dream machine." This photo, taken in 1956, shows the car as it was restyled that year. (Courtesy Joe Bortz).

Calm water greeted these ladies who parked their 1956 Packard Clipper Custom sedan alongside a large lake. On Sept. 24, 1956, a much larger body of water made history when the first telephone cable across the Atlantic Ocean was opened with ceremonies in New York, London and Ottawa.

In response to customer wishes over the years, Packard planned to revive the vertical radiator grille of the prewar era. Appropriately, this was christened the "Packard Request."

Fashion designer Christian Dior died suddenly on Oct. 29, 1957, ending the "Dior Decade." Ladies' styles were moving towards the fitted silhouette look, emphasizing trimness and simplicity. The same could not be said for the chrome-laden 1957 Packard Clipper sedan.

On Sept. 19, 1957 at a sandy proving grounds near Las Vegas, Nevada, the first underground nuclear explosion on record was set off by the Atomic Energy Commission. We hope this lady got her 1957 Packard Clipper sedan out of the sand in time.

Capital expenditures for highway purposes by all levels of government were about $6.2 million in 1958, of which about twenty-nine percent was from federal funds. A 1958 Packard Hawk is seen here near what looks like an almost new viaduct.

This Atlantic Refining Company billboard from the '50s shows a beautiful roadside scene...without billboards. In 1958 — the year this 1958 Packard station wagon was built — Congress voted to control advertising signage along new interstate highways.

Studebaker

In 1950, a bomber-launched VB-3 with a radio set in its tail that sent up a colored flare to guide the bombardier was part of an Air Force display that showed advancements in the guided missiles field. The 1950 Studebaker Land Cruiser sedan looked guided missile-like with its pointed "jet-prow" nose.

Juliette Rochat-Schopfer, a Swiss judge who visited the United States in 1950, noted, "In the American family, the wife comes first, the children second, the family car third and the husband fourth." We have to agree that this woman motorist's 1950 Studebaker Champion convertible is getting the bulk of attention in this photo.

With home construction on the slow side in 1951, this lumberyard worker had time to relax and think about the beauty of his 1951 Studebaker Champion coupe.

Home-building failed to rise in 1951 because curbs on credit, instituted the previous fall as part of postwar economic controls, were holding down new home financing. Material restrictions — due to the Korean conflict buildup — also kept sales of automobiles, such as this 1951 Studebaker Champion Sport coupe, down from the record year 1950.

No one's around in this photo of a 1952 Studebaker Commander Regal coupe. Maybe a Civl Defense "air raid drill" was being conducted. Such drills were well-known to all U.S. citizens in the early 1950s.

An early '50s ad for a Parker Lawn Sweeper may help explain why the lawn in this autumn photograph is so neat. So is the 1952 Studebaker Champion Regal two-door hardtop.

When Studebaker introduced its photogenic 1953 Champion Starlight coupe, astronomers were getting ready to make photographic history. The following year, Dr. E.C. Slipher of Lowell Observatory would snap 10,000 excellent pictures of Mars as the planet made a close approach to the earth.

American Tenley Albright won the senior women's ice skating title in 1953 while Hayes Alan Jenkins captured the men's crown for the first of three consecutive years. Another sporty champion of 1953 was the Studebaker Commander Starliner hardtop.

More than $6.7 billion was spent for building U.S. highways in 1954. Total revenues generated for road building, including bond issue proceeds, were more than $8.2 billion that year. Although the highway beautification program had not started, the 1954 Studebaker Commander Starlight coupe did its part to make this road look better.

Man-made fibers such as dynel or orlon were making fashion news in 1954. They could be woven into cloth for dresses and jackets or into artifical furs. Another fashion hit was the 1954 Studebaker Commander Starliner hardtop.

The United States produced 106 million metric tons of steel during 1955. Much of it went into frames, seen in the background, used for cars such as this Studebaker President Speedster.

ENGINEERS!

Want to explore new frontiers?

Dan'l Boone, Davy C, and those boys of yore would be plumb lost in the frontiers of the sky where Douglas engineers are at home. If you hanker for new

worlds to conquer, write Douglas.

Send resume to **C. C. LaVene, Box 620-E Santa Monica, Calif.**

America's pioneers and settlers were the focus of much attention during the 1950s. One of 1955's top movies was "Oklahoma." The first picture presented in the new "Todd-A-O" system (which joined other '50s photography or projection systems such as Cinerama, CinemaScope, SuperScope and VistaVision), it starred Gordon McRae as Curley and newcomer Shirley Jones as Laurey in the film version of the Rodgers & Hammerstein stage hit. In pioneering spirit, this 1955 Studebaker Commander station wagon was called the "conestoga."

During 1956, the aircraft industry became one of America's largest employers, as every phase of aeronautical activity reached new heights in the nation. These air travelers posed at Bendix Field in South Bend, Indiana with the new 1956 Studebaker Golden Hawk, which sported many aircraft inspired styling motifs.

Coats and jackets with straight lines and buttons were fashionable in 1956. But the trim used on cars, such as this Studebaker President Classic sedan, had few straight lines. Curves and sweeps of chrome — often with contrasting panels — were more commonly seen.

Changes in women's fashions in 1957 included coats curved in an almond-shaped tapered oval with buttons at the throat only and beret-styled hats. This well-dressed model seems proud of her 1957 Studebaker President Classic sedan.

The money spent on new construction in the United States during 1957 rose 2.5 percent to $47.2 billion, but experts said this was due to higher costs rather than more building. Home construction actually dropped $1.1 billion from 1956. This fellow may have paid more to build his home, but his basic, economy-priced 1957 Studebaker "Scotsman" station wagon sold for less than $2,000. It even had painted hubcaps to help keep the price down.

This photo may have been snapped on May 6, 1958, when the fifth annual nationwide civil defense exercise — "Operation Alert 1958" — caused cars to be parked coast-to-coast. The driver of the 1958 Studebaker Silver Hawk might have taken cover when the whistles blew.

Among the 75 new magazine titles appearing in 1958 was **Small Cars Illustrated.** Geared mainly to the compact-sized imports that were selling well during the year's recession, the monthly was unlikely to test drive this 1958 Studebaker President hardtop.

A 1959 billboard extolled the virtues of the Studebaker Lark as a "Fun 'n' Chores" machine. As the photo shows, the new compact was just as suitable for a vacation in Miami Beach, Florida.

New construction grew ten percent in 1959, totaling $54 billion. Many modern new office buildings — such as Corning Glass Work's twenty-eight-story office in New York City with exterior walls of heat-absorbing green glass — were seen in urban areas. Also seen in many urban settings was Studebaker's new compact. This is a 1959 Lark hardtop.

Willys

During 1952, lawyer Allen Davis returned a book that was 26 years and 27 days overdue to the Detroit Public Library. He paid a fine of $162. That same year, Willys-Overland Corporation brought something else it felt was overdue to the American car market. The compact-sized 1952 Willys Eagle proved practical but unpopular in an era when big cars were king.

The French look was in after "Penny" Ridgeway — 33-year-old wife of Gen. Eisenhower's European successor — took over as hostess in Versailles during 1952. The Richmond, Virginia native made national news and sparked interest in French attire. Sporting an equally continental look for this time is the 1952 Willys Aero Wing two-door sedan.

MEN — and Women too!
Get pleasant, vigorous

VIBRATORY MASSAGE
with

**Genuine Battle Creek
HEALTH BUILDER®**

Enjoy the relaxing, stimulating benefits of efficient vibratory massage!
Health Builder gives you pleasant,
scientific deep-tissue manipulation
—"at the snap of a switch." Helps
weight and figure problems, muscle-
toning, blood circulation. *Widely
used in Health institutions.* Built
for years of service—fully guaran-
teed. WRITE today for literature
and new booklet. "BE GOOD TO
YOURSELF!"

Battle Creek
EQUIPMENT CO.
Battle Creek 30, Mich.

Weight control was a problem in the fabulous '50s, too. Americans relied on machines like the "Health Builder" to shed pounds. Willys-Overland accomplished the same goal by building small cars. This is the 1954 Ace Deluxe sedan.

The new for 1954 Willys line was introduced in February of that year (not in the fall of 1953). This is the 1954 Lark Deluxe two-door sedan outside a movie theater. Wonder what was featured on the marquee?

GRASS CUTTING

1950
style
WITH A JACOBSEN
POWER
MOWER

JACOBSEN
LAWN
QUEEN

20-inch cutting width $127.50
22-inch cutting width $137.50
Plus Freight

Zip through grass cutting the easy, no-push way. Quick-starting Jacobsen engine snaps into action — gives you extra power for heavy growths, hillside cutting. Eight power mower models starting at $99.50.

Jacobsen Racine, Wisconsin

MANUFACTURING
COMPANY

An ad for a 1950 Jacobsen power mower illustrates the type of machine that may have been used to trim the lawn under this early 1955 Willys Ace Deluxe four-door sedan.

By the end of 1955, mechanical and electrical costs were about thirty percent of the cost of a home, a big increase from the past. The electric yard lamp seen here illustrates the many more electric conveniences that were being used in or around American homes. Shown here is a 1955 Willys Custom four-door sedan.

Industrial design was a young and blossoming industry during the fabulous '50s. One of the field's pioneers was Brooks Stevens, seen here in a prototype Willys Jeepster designed for the late 1950s South American export market.

During the '50s, automobile styling studios were mysterious places where creative geniuses shaped "cars of the future." This is the Brooks Stevens Association design center, near Milwaukee, with a Willys project underway. Styling models, such as those seen in the background, are valuable '50s collectibles today.

Brooks Stevens poses with one of his redesigns of the Willys for the South American market. After Willys-Overland dropped its passenger car line in mid-1955, the body dies were sent to a Kaiser Industries subsidiary — Willys de Brasil — which continued building and selling the cars until 1962.

Collector's Corner
Chrysler Corporation

This 1955 Chrysler New Yorker Deluxe Newport two-door hardtop, owned by Terry Hoeman of Columbus, Nebraska, was recently purchased by Hoeman in Colorado. The car is black and white with a gold and white interior.

Mark Waite of Eau Claire, Wisconsin is the proud owner of this 1952 DeSoto Firedome, which features a V-8 engine available for the first time in a DeSoto.

This 1952 Plymouth Savoy occupies a special place in the hearts of owners Bill and Pat Morton of Bellevue, Nebraska. The sleek Savoy joined the Morton family on the same day and almost the same hour as a grandson!

Harvey and Gayle Pagel, of Delafield, Wisconsin, are proud of their 1955 Plymouth Belvedere Sport Coupe. This car sat in a tobacco barn in Paradise, Pennsylvania, for ten years before they bought and restored it!

Hastings, Nebraska's own Willard Stein has a gem of a car. The 1955 Plymouth Belvedere Sport Coupe was voted the "most beautiful car of the year" by the Society of Illustrations.

New Hampshire's Richard D. Welch owns this 1956 Plymouth Fury. According to Welch, the numbers match on engine, transmission and body.

Tom Mitchell's 1958 Plymouth Fury spent most of its life in the Sacramento, California area. After 1968, it was parked inside with just 39,110 miles on it. The gem now resides with Mitchell in Columbia, Missouri.

Gary Behling, of Milwaukee, shows off his 1959 Plymouth Sport Fury convertible, an all-original, 37,000-mile car. Behling says he bought the Plymouth because it is an "exact copy of my first car, which I owned in 1966 when I was eighteen."

George and Bea Dalinis of Wilmington, Illinois purchased this 1959 Plymouth Sport Fury, which had been stored in a garage for twenty years and had only 4,000 miles on it!

Ford Motor Company

The 1959 Edsel is one of the most easily recognized 1950s vehicles because of its horse-collar grille. This Ranger belongs to Kilian Ashbeck of Wisconsin Rapids, Wisconsin.

Robert A. and Margaret Fisher's 1950 Ford V-8 Custom Deluxe Club Coupe is driven 500-750 miles yearly, according to the River Falls, Wisconsin couple. Of his three collector Fords, Fisher prefers this one.

This 1950 Ford is the same kind of car owner Thomas E. Strak of Racine, Wisconsin had 30 years ago when he and his wife got married.

"Ol' Blue" is the moniker Wes and Betty Campbell, Wauwatosa, Wisconsin, gave their 1953 Ford Customline four-door sedan, which has been in the Campbell family for years.

This example of Ford's 50th anniversary truck — the 1953 F-100 — belongs to Jerome Scray of Green Bay, Wisconsin, who's owned the snazzy vehicle for 17 years.

This 1953 Ford Customline two-door sedan belonging to Les and Shirley Abraham of Green Bay, Wisconsin, has plates originally issued to the car in 1953.

This picture of a 1955 Ford Country Squire was shot at Iola '87. J. D. Schmitt of Waukesha, Wisconsin owns this station wagon, which he purchased on Aug. 23, 1955.

This 1955 Ford Fairlane Victoria belongs to Donna and Jon Vollmer of Kaukauna, Wisconsin. It will be part of the Iola '92 car show, which features cars from the 1950s.

Donald A. Severson's 1955 Ford Fairlane Crown Victoria has new paint and matching red and white interior. The Prescott, Wisconsin resident says the car was restored and has matching numbers on the data plate.

This 1956 Ford Sunliner convertible was hauled from northern Wisconsin to Portage, Wisconsin by owner Wayne Johnson of Portage. The car's condition upon purchase gave new meaning to the words "basket case," Johnson says, but three-and-a-half years later, his dream was finally complete.

James L. Johnston of Windsor, Wisconsin, bought this 1957 Ford Thunderbird from a Ford Motor Company executive, who was its second owner. According to Johnston, this was the 151st from last 1957 T-bird produced on the assembly line.

This 1957 Ford retractable had a frame-off restoration, inside and out, according to Harold Tyson of Ceresco, Michigan.

Randy Rostecki's 1959 Ford Fairlane 500 convertible was built on Nov. 14, 1958 at the Kansas City Ford plant. The Winnipeg, Manitoba man says he bought the Ford from a salvage yard near Denver in 1978; the car's restoration took six years.

George M. Lucie Jr.'s 1954 Lincoln Capri sedan recently turned 60,000 miles. Last year, the car took ten trophies in fourteen shows in Illinois and Wisconsin, the Chicago man said.

This 1958 Lincoln Continental Mark III convertible was known as the "ultimate land yacht," according to owner Bud Waite of Eau Claire, Wisconsin.

Heinz Diehl's 1950 Mercury will be part of Iola '92. Diehl will bring the car from Greendale, Wisconsin.

Even with Mt. Rushmore as a dramatic backdrop, this 1951 Mercury convertible is still an eye-catcher. The car, which belongs to Laurence D. Suhsen of Delano, Minnesota, gets 2,000 miles added to it every summer.

Guy and Sharon Buswell's 1951 Mercury four-door sedan is an example of the era of Mercury that was popularized by actor James Dean. This Mercury is the body style of choice for customizing, and it's unusual to find one in original condition.

This 1953 Mercury Monterey two-door hardtop belongs to Jerome P. Bergdorf of West Bend, Wisconsin. The car has its original flathead V-8 and three-speed with overdrive transmission. It also sports a factory visor, fog lights, dual exhausts and power steering.

This 1957 Mercury Turnpike Cruiser is owned by Bill Konieczny of Chicago. The exterior is original, but the interior has been redone with all correct material.

General Motors

Robert "Pinky" Williams, Chatham, Illinois, says his 1953 Buick Skylark has won many awards, including an Antique Automobile Club of America 1st Senior and 1st Junior, Grand National 1st and Milestone Cup.

This 1957 Cadillac Fleetwood 60 Special four-door hardtop belonging to Robert A. Henke of Nekoosa, Wisconsin has 73,000 actual miles on its odometer. "This beautiful machine has been kept in Wisconsin since new," Henke says. "We have had it at Iola every year since 1978."

This 1950 Chevrolet Bel Air two-door hardtop owned by Roger Davidson has many options: compass, spotlight with mirror, bumper wing tips, clock and cigar lighter, among others.

This 1950 Chevy Deluxe four-door has had a lot of body work done to it, according to Dousman, Wisconsin resident Dean A. Diedrich. The car has about 44,000 actual miles "and drives very well," he says.

"Cherry Pie," a customized 1951 Chevy Bel Air hardtop, has a red and white "tuck 'n' roll" interior and has won twelve first place trophies out of thirteen car shows, according to owner Aileen Hyke of Rochester, Minnesota.

Gordon Jacobson, of Plymouth, Wisconsin, will be heading to Iola '92's "Fabulous '50s" show with his 1952 Chevy Bel Air two-door hardtop.

Donald Desing's 1952 Chevy Bel Air two-door hardtop has been restored and has won an Antique Automobile Club of America National 1st and a Senior 1st. "The car is absolutely correct," the Janesville, Wisconsin man says.

This 1955 Chevy Bel Air two-door hardtop belongs to Edward K. Reavie, who runs the giant Straits Area Antique Auto Show in St. Ignace, Michigan every June.

"I have owned many cars, but this is my favorite," says Deems D. Pelishek, who owns this 1956 Chevy Nomad. "During the summer, I drive the car almost daily."

This 1956 Chevy Bel Air convertible, which belongs to Larry Boe of Brookfield, Wisconsin, has been part of Iola's "Blue Ribbon Concours" for the past six years. The car has been restored and detailed throughout.

Jackson Taylor, of Green Lake, Wisconsin, is proud of his 1958 Chevy Bel Air two-door hardtop with factory continental kit. This car was discovered in Nashville by a Wisconsin couple honeymooning on their motorcycle. The bride got to drive the car home!

This 1959 Chevy Impala, owned by James E. Peters of Mequon, Wisconsin, is a beautiful car with 42,000 original miles.

This was car No. 340 off the assembly line on Oct. 24, 1957, but when owner Dennis U. Krause of Wisconsin found this '58 Corvette, it was a basket case. "From that ugly duckling to the car you see in my photo was quite an adventure," he says.

This unrestored 1950 Oldsmobile two-door Sedan Deluxe has only 17,000 original miles. It belongs to Wayne Holous of Lemont, Illinois.

Ed Servais' 1950 Oldsmobile Holiday two-door hardtop, model 76, has one of the last flathead big six engines produced. Servais will bring his Olds to Iola from DePere, Wisconsin.

Wayne Holous, of Lemont, Illinois, is proud of his 1950 Oldsmobile two-door Club Sedan Deluxe, as the license plate indicates.

Richard Fleury of Green Bay, Wisconsin, bought this beautiful 1954 Oldsmobile Super 88 from an advertiser in **Old Cars Weekly.** *Fleury's first set of wheels also was a 1954 Olds Super 88 that he bought in 1965.*

Nineteen-year-old Jason Fridley owns this 1958 Oldsmobile Super 88 two-door hardtop, which came from South Dakota. Fridley added lake pipes on the side and chrome megaphone exhausts on the rear, and would truly love to make the car a complete low-rider.

This 1950 Pontiac Silver Streak, which belongs to Wayne Holous of Lemont, Illinois, has an eight-cylinder engine and 35,000 original miles.

Fabulous '50s *co-editor John Gunnell of Iola, Wisconsin, has such confidence in his 1953 Pontiac Catalina that he's taken it on trips halfway across the country.*

John Krempasky, of Madison, Wisconsin, calls his 1957 Pontiac Star Chief convertible "super sharp." We agree!

1958 was the first year for the Pontiac Bonneville Sport Coupe. This sparkling beauty belongs to Bob and Marlene Peterson of Burnettsville, Indiana.

Independents

This 1955 Kaiser Manhattan is reportedly the last Kaiser built, according to owners James and Glee Westfall of Harville, Ohio. This last car off the assembly line in Toledo is totally unrestored with 41,575 original miles.

*It's not a bunny, but this 1955 Nash Rambler Country Club, which belongs to Gordon Gochenaur of Richland Center, Wisconsin, was pictured in the April 1990 issue of **Playboy** magazine.*

This 1959 Rambler Ambassador Super four-door is owned by Lief Hillesland of Crivitz, Wisconsin. Hillesland says he's been to Iola every year since 1987, and will return for 1992.

This completely stock 1955 Studebaker Commander Regal two-door hardtop has won several trophies, including first place in its class at the Studebaker Nationals in Springfield, Missouri in 1991, according to owner Robert Christianson of Union Grove, Wisconsin.

This 1955 Packard Caribbean convertible will be at Iola '92. It is owned by Eric Yeley of McCordsville, Indiana.

This 1957 Ward LaFrance fire truck once belonged to the Fond du Lac, Wisconsin Fire Department, but now Frank and Mary Quick of that city are the proud owners. The fire department bought the truck new and used it until it was retired in 1990. Now it does the parade-and-party circuit!

ATTENTION CAR FANS...

When you can't be at the auction, turn to...

OLD CARS WEEKLY NEWS & MARKETPLACE

Get the latest auction results every week, plus restoration tips, car show calendar, vehicle profiles and America's most up-to-date marketplace with thousands of cars and parts for sale!

26 ISSUES
Only $15.75

When you need to know the value, turn to...

OLD CARS PRICE GUIDE

Get up-to-date collector car values in six conditional grades -- over 130,000 prices per issue -- for most cars manufactured from 1901-1985!

6 ISSUES
Only $16.95

MASTERCARD / VISA CARDHOLDERS CALL TOLL-FREE TO ORDER

(800) 258-0929 Dept. 7WE

Mon.-Fri. 6:30 am-8:00 pm, Sat. 8:00 am-2:00 pm, CST

OUTSTANDING CATALOGS

$45.00

$24.95

$24.95

$24.95

$19.95

krause publications
700 E. State St., Iola, WI 54990 715/445-2214

MASTERCARD / VISA CARDHOLDERS

FOR VEHICLE ENTHUSIASTS

standard catalog of
FORD
1903-1990

Complete coverage
FORD
MERCURY
EDSEL
LINCOLN
MUSTANG

$19.95

standard catalog of
CHEVROLET
1912-1990

Complete coverage
CHEVROLET
CORVETTE
CAMARO
CORVAIR

$19.95

standard catalog of
CHRYSLER
1924-1990

Complete coverage
CHRYS
DODG
PLYMO
DESO
IMPER

$19.95

standard catalog of
BUICK
1903-1990

$18.95

standard catalog of
CADILLAC
1903-1990

$18.95

krause
publications
700 E. State St., Iola, WI 54990 715/445-2214

CALL TOLL-FREE
TO ORDER...
800-258-0929

Dept. ZGN
Mon.-Fri. 7 am-8 pm
Sat. 8 am - 2 pm, CST

UNIQUE AUTOMOTIVE REFERENCES

Standard Guide to AUTOMOTIVE RESTORATION
Matt Joseph "On Restoration"
- A Practical Approach to Car Restoration
- All Makes, All Models, All Years
- Step-By-Step Hows & Whys
- Arranged by Automotive System
- Strategies, Procedures & Practices
- Over 400 Photos & Illustrations

Selected photography by Joseph W. Jackson III

$24.95

standard guide to Cars & Prices 4th EDITION
1901-1984
CURRENT PRICES FOR 1993 IN 6 GRADES
- ORIGINAL MODELS
- SELECTED SPORTS CARS, IMPORTS, & LIGHT TRUCKS
- MORE THAN 150 PHOTOS FOR MODEL IDENTIFICATION

$14.95

The Fabulous '50s
The Cars, the Culture
Edited by John A. Gunnell & Mary L. Sieber

$14.95

Police Cars
A Photographic History
by Monty McCord

$14.95

ANTIQUE CAR WRECKS
From Old Cars Weekly's "Wreck of the Week" photo album
OVER 200 SELECTED PHOTOS

$14.95

kp krause publications
700 E. State St., Iola, WI 54990 715/445-2214

MASTERCARD / VISA ORDERS CALL TOLL-FREE...
800-258-0929
Dept. ZGN
Mon.-Fri. 7 am-8 pm
Sat. 8 am - 2 pm, CST